FULL SEASON ACADEMY TRAINING PROGRAM

U13-15

48 Sessions (245 Practices) from Italian Series 'A' Coaches

WRITTEN BY

MIRKO MAZZANTINI & SIMONE BOMBARDIERI

PUBLISHED BY

FULL SEASON ACADEMY TRAINING PROGRAM
U13-15

48 Sessions (245 Practices) from Italian Series 'A' Coaches

First Published July 2013 by SoccerTutor.com
Info@soccertutor.com | www.SoccerTutor.com
UK: 0208 1234 007 | **US:** (305) 767 4443 | **ROTW:** +44 208 1234 007
ISBN: 978-0-9576705-2-5

Authors
Mirko Mazzantini and Simone Bombardieri © 2013

Edited by
Alex Fitzgerald - SoccerTutor.com

Cover Design by
Alex Macrides, Think Out Of The Box Ltd.
Email: design@thinkootb.com Tel: +44 (0) 208 144 3550

Diagrams
Diagram designs by SoccerTutor.com. All the diagrams in this book have been created using SoccerTutor.com Tactics Manager Software available from *www.SoccerTutor.com*

Note: While every effort has been made to ensure the technical accuracy of the content of this book, neither the author nor publishers can accept any responsibility for any injury or loss sustained as a result of the use of this material.

Soccer Italian Style Coaches

Mirko Mazzantini
ACF Fiorentina
Academy Coach

Mirko Mazzantini coached at Empoli FC for 10 years, working with all the main age groups at academy level. In 2010 he was recruited by AFC Fiorentina to work with the U14/U15 Academy teams.

During the 2010/11 season Mirko won the U15 Italian Academy Serie 'A' championship.

In 2011/12 Mirko was the Assistant of the Fiorentina Reserve team during pre-season and he was the coach of the ACF Fiorentina U14 team who won the Academy Serie 'A' championship and some international tournaments.

Mirko is currently the ACF Fiorentina U15 coach for the 2012/13 season.

He is a qualified football coach through the "Young Players Coach" program and a UEFA 'B' Licenced Coach, as well as an author of many coaching publications, articles, books and DVDs.

Simone Bombardieri
Empoli FC
Academy Coach

Simone Bombardieri played for Empoli FC for 5 years. He then started his career as a coach for the club 15 years ago at the age of 22, where he has been coaching various academy age groups from U9-U14.

In the 2011/12 season, Simone was the coach of the Empoli FC U14 team who reached the final of the Nick Cup International Tournament, where they lost in extra time against Inter Milan. They also finished eighth in the Academy Serie 'A' championship.

Simone is currently the Empoli FC U15 coach for the 2012/13 season.

He is also a qualified football coach through the "Young Players Coach" program and a UEFA 'B' Licenced Coach, as well as an author of many coaching publications, articles, books and DVDs.

Tommaso Tanini
ACF Fiorentina
Academy Coach

We would like to give a special thanks to Tommaso Tanini for helping us produce this book. Tommaso has coached at Empoli FC for 11 years. Tommaso is now the Fitness Coach for the Fiorentina U15 team.

He is also a UEFA 'B' Licenced Coach.

Soccer Italian Style

SOCCER ITALIAN STYLE IS WORLDWIDE...WORK WITH US!

SOCCER ITALIAN STYLE has organised youth football events in many countries around the world. If you are a Club Executive, a Coach, a Technical Director or just an individual passionate about the sport and you want your players to have a unique experience, please contact us or visit our website: www. SoccerItalianStyle.it

PROFESSIONAL ITALIAN CAMP is a week of football for boys and girls aged 6 to 18 years old. It is where fun meets the training methodologies of the best Italian academies and is taught by experienced staff who have worked with with some of highest level clubs in Italy.

PROFESSIONAL ITALIAN TEAM CAMP is a weekly team training camp with the work planned around a highly professional methodology which is tested continuously, innovated and adapted based on the level and characteristics of the participating team.

SOCCER ITALIAN STYLE COACHING CLINICS are organised for all different levels and are based on a proven model that creates lots of interest and enjoyment for the participants. The time spent in the classroom is filled with numerous videos from professional training sessions in Italy and it is supported by on-field demonstrations of the concepts discussed.

NEW INITIATIVE: SOCCER AND TOURISM IN ITALY: Soccer Italian Style has a partnership with an important travel agency to provide a unique experience: improve as a player and sightsee the best parts of Tuscany. Firenze, Pisa, Lucca, Siena, and 5 Terre are just some of the magnificent places waiting for you.

If you want your team to have a week of highly professional training and at the same time be immersed in the culture of Italy, Soccer Italian Style can plan your trip in detail, adapting the itinerary and lodging based on the wishes and needs of the players and chaperones.

The Italian Style Story

Soccer Italian Style was founded in 2005 by 2 passionate professional coaches, Mirko Mazzantini and Simone Bombardieri. Since their first trip overseas, the young coaches' goal has been to share their experiences with passion and professionalism.

The Soccer Italian Style network has spread quickly to many continents through various partnerships, working with youth football clubs, youth football associations and businesses that distribute sports books and videos.

In 2011 Mirko Mazzantini and Simone Bombarideri had the honour to present a lesson at the Coverciano Coaches Training Centre organised by the Italian Football Federation.

Mirko and Simone have received recognition from many countries, and this is reflected in themany contacts and collaborations they have established and by the success of the products developed. This has led to Mirko and Simone visiting many countries throughout the world to share their expertise, particularly in the USA, Canada, Norway, Japan, Australia, New Zealand and many Asian countries. The success enjoyed by Soccer Italian Style has encouraged the founders to increase their efforts with new developments to complement the existing products.

All the initiatives focus on the common denominator; the working philosophy of Soccer Italian Style, as well as the result of personal experiences in professional football clubs, trips around the world and personal experiences.

Numerous coaches, club directors and football fans continuously contact the staff through the website:

www.SoccerItalianStyle.it

As a result of this interest, Mirko and Simone have welcomed other professional coaches and athletic trainers to their football family to help meet the needs of all that are interested.

Contents

CONTENTS

Introduction

This book focuses on the principal characteristics of players between the age of 12 and 15, which is a very important period in the psychological and physical growth of players.

The objective of this book is to share our training methodology, which focuses on developing technical skills, while at the same time devoting the adequate time to teach the fundamentals of individual tactics and group tactics.

It is important at this age to start working on developing the tactical thought, which will improve and increase during the player's growth.

The book will also focus on motor and coordination skills and the fundamental aspects of conditioning.

The objective of each session is to develop the technical aspect (by way of an initial warm up game and or a technical activity) the motor and physical aspect (by way of a coordination or conditional activity) and an individual tactical aspect (by way of a game situation or specific games).

The book will also introduce the first concepts of group tactics based around the 4-4-2 system of play.

PHYSICAL AND PSYCHOLOGICAL CHARACTERISTICS AND ELEMENTS OF TRAINING METHODOLOGY

Growth Maturation: Physical Growth

It is important for the coach of this age level to understand the maturation process of the body the players go through.

Mr. Goding and Mr. Stratz have studied this maturation and developed 3 fundamental principals on which the body maturation is based.

Stratz states there are alternating phases between weight and height.

The alternating periods start with the 'turgor primis' stage (2-4 years old) in which the body gains weight and the body structure assumes a more round shape.

The second phase is the 'proceritas prima' (5-7 years old) with an increase in height.

The third phase (8-10 years old for girls and until 11 for boys) is called 'turgor secundus' which is characterised by another increase in body weight and an increase in power, muscle tone and general coordination.

The fourth phase, which is the phase we are focusing on (11-13 years old) is called 'proceritas secunda' and it is marked by a general transformation of the size and characteristics of the player.

In this period we note the increase in the length of the limbs, in the height and in the weight with a slight loss of coordination.

The psychological aspect is also affected with the change of voice among other aspects of change during the puberty process.

The fifth phase 'turgor tertius' (14-17 years old for boys and 13-16 for girls) is marked by an increase in the hormone activity and a slow down in the growth of the bone structure.

The sixth phase 'proceritas tertia' (17-21 for boys and 15-18 for girls) and finally the seventh phase

'turgus quartus' (19-21) conclude the physical growth of the individual.

Godin instead states there are shorter periods in which the body alternates phases of growth in length and phases of growth in width of the long bones such as the legs and arms.

Therefore a limb undergoes periods in which its length is increased and periods in which its diameter is growing.

Mr. Godin also states that in the 2 semesters prior to puberty, the lengthening of the limbs coincides with an increase in height of the individual, and in the 2 semesters post puberty we witness an increase in weight.

It is also important to note in the post-puberty period the muscle tone has a relevant increase and in the prepuberty period there is an important increase in the length of the leg bones.

Conditioning

STRENGTH

Strength is the ability to contrast and/or win against an external resistance.

The resistance can be from your own body (jumping), from a part of the body (raise your leg), or from an external load (a push of from opponents).

Many factors affect the strength of an individual:

- Muscle volume
- Neuromuscular quality of the muscle fibres
- Genetic factors
- Nervous impulse frequency
- Gender
- Availability of energetic resources

Muscle Volume

Strength is proportional to the volume of the muscle, so the larger the muscle the larger the strength.

Neuromuscular Quality of the Muscle Fibres

There are red and white fibres. The red fibres have more resistant characteristics and stabilise the movements. The white fibres instead contract faster and with more intensity.

Genetic Factors

Hereditary factors associated with ethnic background have an effect on the strength of an individual.

Gender

Until puberty with the same rate of training, force is identical in males and females. After puberty the force of a male and a female differs due to the different characteristics of the genders.

There are 2 types of strength:

Absolute and Relative strength.

Absolute strength is the strength an athlete is able to express regardless of their weight.

Relative strength is the relationship between the absolute strength and the weight of the individual.

Who has more absolute strength and who has more relative strength between 2 athletes who can lift 1000 Kg and weigh 70 Kg and 90 Kg?

From a mechanical point of view, when a force is applied there is the movement, acceleration (A) of a mass (M): therefore the intensity (F) of the force to apply is the product of the mass time acceleration ($F = M \times A$).

There are different types of muscle strength applied to a sport gesture:

- Maximal, fast, resistant
- Maximal strength or pure strength

It is the maximum tension developed by a voluntary muscle contraction to win a resistance. It depends on the volume and the quantity of fibres that make the muscle mass.

Maximal strength can be trained and requires a significant effort but it should not be trained before the compete development of the skeleton-muscle system.

This should not to be trained before the ages of 16 or 17 years old.

Speed Strength or Power

The ability to develop strength of high intensity in the shortest time frame.

Strength Endurance

It is the ability to sustain a workload of relative strength for a certain period of time.

Training Strength At this Level

Depending on the sport and the type of strength training, sessions are specific and designed with the individual in mind.

This ability, if trained, can be improved significantly. On the other hand, if the muscle is not trained it will lose muscle tone and the strength itself.

As discussed earlier, until the full sexual maturation (approximately 14 years old) we should not talk about training maximal strength with weights and specific weight machines, because the intervention would be negative on the delicate and unstable bone structures.

Even from a psychological point of view a boring and monotonous type of training like weight lifting is not adequate for an age always in search of motivation and with a low rate of concentration.

Activities to train this ability are fun circuit training, motivational and stimulating activities which alternate technical/motor gestures and exercises with natural weight loads.

If we want to train the athlete for weight lifting it is important to teach the proper technique, with the positioning of the lower limbs and good posture.

It is very important to exercise care if the athlete is subject to weight lifting before 14 or 15 year old, unless the individual is blessed with a reasonable general condition and a decent abdominal, dorsal and pectoral muscle mass.

However, even if the athlete is blessed with a good physical structure it is important to follow the fundamental rules during the weight activities:

- Warm up before the work

- Never lift excess weights that only allow 1 lift

- Never hold a weight for a long time

- Teach the proper posture and breathing

- Always perform stretching after the activity

The type of strength mostly trained at the age of 14 and 15 is the speed strength and the strength endurance.

The inclusion in the group is very important in this period. It is through the participation within groups that adolescents can find their social identity.

Being in groups allows adolescents to get to know themselves and others. He or she can learn to deal with individuals of the opposite sex in a protected environment.

They can relate to older friends who have the same interests and consider them role models (more so than with an adult).

The social game becomes important. With the development of the formal thought, adolescents are able to play games with more complex rules, like cards and chess.

And sports have the function of enjoyment, allowing the individual to live, even if at a symbolic level, the problems and conflicts arising in day to day life.

Sport can be very important for an individual for social challenges, and by means for the formation and control of their identity.

Speed Strength

This is trained with activities with a natural weight load, with constant movements at adequate speed. The repetitions should not be higher than 8-10 and the series between 3-5.

This is because the workload must be sharp and the muscle fibres should not tire.

Speed strength means speed and power of the muscle. Ply metrics is a methodology that uses the elastic strength accumulated by the muscle after a contraction.

Strength Endurance

In football, it is important to maintain an adequate level of strength even when the muscle starts to tire.

Strength endurance is trained with slow repetitions where significant resistance is applied for a longer period of time.

The progression of this activity is characterised by an increment of the time the activity is performed.

The number of repetitions can be 18-20 and the loads should be between 30-60% of the maximum. Recovery between the 3-5 series cannot be lower than 45 seconds.

The speed of execution of the exercises must be moderate.

Circuit training with stations, with the introduction of the ball and the technical gesture is probably the best type of training to stimulate concentration and enjoyment.

ENDURANCE

It is the motor conditional skills that allow the player to extend the workload despite getting tired.

Endurance is connected to the quantity of red muscle fibres, to the functionality of the circulatory and respiratory systems that generate energy to sustain the aerobic, anaerobic a-lactic and anaerobic lactic workload.

To train endurance we need to wait for the full development of those systems which happens at around 14 years old.

Endurance can be general and specific.

General endurance does not depend on the type of activity but depends on the aerobic capacity and the capillarity or the capacity of the blood cells to supply oxygen to the muscles.

Specific endurance is specific to the activity performed by the individual.

The time of exercise should not be excessive because the exercises must be performed at a medium intensity. Recovery times are proportional to the workload.

To train this ability we can opt for mixed activities with or without the ball, ie. circuits, relays.

Ball possession, situation games and small sided games are preferred to runs and laps around the field.

In the event the field is not playable we can adopt a fartlek (interval training) type of running, with changes of speed and rhythm.

SPEED

Speed represents the relationship between space and the time needed to travel. Therefore if 2 athletes run a 100 metre race, the fastest is the one who finishes first.

In football speed is a very important conditional skill, but this must be combined with control of the ball. A football player must have a good degree of basic speed but he must first be reactive and explosive, with a great sense of timing and powerful over short distances with a great ability to accelerate at the right moment with an effective change of pace.

The players must also be quick and comfortable while running with the ball, a fundamental technical skill.

It has been evident for some time now that the methodology of training a track and field athlete is used to train speed in football. There is a pure speed without the ball (a motor conditional skill) and a speed while in possession of the ball (a technical ability).

The pure speed is effected by the genetics of an individual and the quantity of white fibres in the muscles of an athlete.

With proper training we can intervene on the efficiency of the nervous system and on the functionality of the muscle system.

In order to plan our training sessions we must consider that speed starts to develop early between the ages of 1 and 6, with the possibility to transform the slow red muscle fibres into fast white fibres (between 13 and 15 years old) before puberty, even if in small proportions.

We must train to improve the speed of reactions, the sprinting abilities, the acceleration and the integration of these 3 elements that together form the speed of covering the distance required in the least amount of time. For this the psychokinetic is a methodology used a lot in football.

All the exercises that involve a stimulus and a reaction (various commands & various types of feedback - audio, visual etc), if they are properly planned, provided and performed can improve in the shortest time the quality of reaction to the stimulus and the kinetic reaction directly proportional to the functionality of the nervous system.

From 12 to 15 years old, the acceleration can be trained and improved significantly.

The use of the ball in these type of training is important as well as the 'dry exercises' (without the ball) can be useful. For example, a game between 2 players who must sprint and accelerate for 15 yards after a visual or audio command and then shoot at goal at the end is a fine example of what we mean.

When the strength speed and the general mobility is trained and improved we also intervene in a positive way on the ability to perform motor acts faster and quicker. The principle for the specific training of pure speed is to plan exercises of short duration, with a maximum of 10 seconds at the maximum speed and with medium/long recovery times to allow the muscle and the brain to restore its freshness and sharpness.

QUICKNESS

Speed is not synonymous for quickness. This skill represents the ability to perform one or more motor gestures in the shortest time.

A guitarist moves his finger quickly while playing a song, just like a striker can be quick in performing combined gestures of dribbling and shooting even if he does not possess a high speed base.

We need to be careful when we plan sessions, to think that speed is the athletic objective and instead the exercises work on quickness, or vice versa.

AGILITY AND MOBILITY

In the last 10 years literature considers this ability between conditional and coordination skills. Agility represents the ability to perform gestures with the maximum agility and flexibility.

The structural and physiological properties, the joint of the newborn and children are more flexible then the adults. Cartilage rather than bones, greater ligament flexibility and low muscle tone, are factors in favour of the younger individuals.

The age we are working with poses a challenge since the athletes undergo an increase in muscle tone and in strength limiting the flexibility and agility of the player.

Therefore it is important that in training we devote some time to the flexibility and general mobility through 3 methodologies: active exercise, passive exercise and stretching. Certainly the first method is the one to favour with dynamic exercises, however even stretching has its relevance and must be included in the training schedule of the coach or trainer.

Coordination Skills

As already discussed between the ages of 5 and 12 coordination skills develop at a faster rate. In the age we are analysing (12-15) coordination skills are subject to a slowdown in the development and need to adjust to compensate for the increase in body length and the proportion between the torso and the arms and the torso and the legs.

Dexterity for example is the coordination ability that by 12 years has completely developed.

Coordination skills are usually divided into general coordination skills and special coordination skills.

General Coordination Skills:

- Skill of motor learning
- Skill of motor control
- Skill of transformation and adaptation

The first skill allows the acquisition of new gestures that stabilise through correction and repetition of the gesture.

The second skill allows controlling the gesture and movement depending on the target.

The third skill allows transforming and adapting the movements to the different situations that evolve from time to time.

Special Coordination Skills:

- Dexterity
- Skill of combining various gestures together
- Reaction skill
- Skill of dynamic differentiation, allowing the analysis of data originating from outside and adequate motor reaction.
- Skill of temporal differentiation allowing to give order of sequence to the motor process. In football, the study of this skill is very important to learn the trajectory, the distance, the direction and speed of the ball.
- Skill of motor anticipation

- Skill of motor creativity
- Skill of orientation allowing to use space properly
- Skill and expression of rhythm in the motor gestures (e.g. the gesture of a goalkeeper that prepares himself to catch a high ball).
- Balance

BALANCE

The balance as a coordination skill and its development and training deserve particular attention.

Balance is the skill to maintain stability of the body during the various situations both static and dynamic.

The relevance of balance in football is very evident. In fact a player that is able to restore their balance quickly after a tackle, after heading the ball or after shooting, has more opportunities to manage subsequent movements and technical skills effectively.

Balance is directly related to the centre of gravity. Generally a body is in balance when the imaginary line from the centre of gravity to the ground falls inside the standing base which is the space between the feet.

On the contrary if that line falls outside the base the body is not in balance. This is why it is evident that a player with a low centre of gravity has more balance when moving with the ball.

Balance can be static when the individual does not move and the centre of gravity does not move. Balance can be dynamic when the centre of gravity changes continually with movement. Balance can be in the air when the athlete does not have their feet on the ground.

For training coordination skills and balance, it is necessary to plan and prepare activities full of creativity. Exercises used in other sports are the foundation for a complete development of a wide motor memory.

Circuit training, requiring agility and the ability to change from one position to another, from a type of balance to another are necessary for an effective training program.

PSYCHOLOGY FOR 12-15 YEAR OLDS

According to Freud this age group is characterised by the sexual organisation and sublimation modifying the natural expression of an impulse or instinct (especially a sexual one) to one that is socially acceptable.

Males show signs of more aggressiveness. They favour games with rules and social games, therefore football is a great answer to this need.

There is a valorisation of 'myself' as the individual forms their own personality, values and feelings. At this age there is a movement to the full development of a proper identity.

Parents and teachers are now are criticised. Their defects are magnified and the coach can become a reference point.

In this stage there is also the formation of intimacy. Therefore, we need to pay attention because even if the coach is well respected and followed, his honesty of thought and his behaviour is continually tested and analysed by the adolescent.

From a social aspect, these years are important because the individuals find mental support with each other.

Therefore their football team has a sense of belonging, acceptance and integration.

The 12 - 15 years olds find great support in their team and use the group as a means to get feedback and experiment their self expression.

Therefore, the sport of football for the individual at this age has a big impact for the rest of their life.

For a social aspect, for the performance in school, for the overall health of the individual and his involvement with other activities, football can be a key element of their lives.

Dropping out from the sport is a draw back at this age and the cause can often be a bad relationship with the coach, possibly due to a lack of fun elements in training sessions and games.

Therefore, it is important that the coach improvises and also has an awareness of the psychological aspects of training teenage players.

This is added to the ability to coach the technical and tactical fundamentals.

TRAINING SESSION FORMAT

Outline of Training Sessions

The 45 sessions are organised into weekly training blocks based on 3 training sessions per week. In order to allow the players to learn more efficiently, it is advised that each training block should be practiced for at least 2 weeks (repeating the same sessions the second week). There will obviously be exceptions and changes if the coach wanted to work on specific topics.

This full season training program produces 30 weeks of training (based on 3 sessions per week).

This training program has been implemented in Italian Serie 'A' academy teams with great success. We also have 20 additional practices on strength, endurance and speed at the end of this book to implement into the sessions where you see fit.

WEEK 1	Sessions 1, 2 & 3		WEEK 16	Sessions 22, 23 & 24
WEEK 2	Sessions 1, 2 & 3		WEEK 17	Sessions 25, 26 & 27
WEEK 3	Sessions 4, 5 & 6		WEEK 18	Sessions 25, 26 & 27
WEEK 4	Sessions 4, 5 & 6		WEEK 19	Sessions 28, 29 & 30
WEEK 5	Sessions 7, 8 & 9		WEEK 20	Sessions 28, 29 & 30
WEEK 6	Sessions 7, 8 & 9		WEEK 21	Sessions 31, 32 & 33
WEEK 7	Sessions 10, 11 & 12		WEEK 22	Sessions 31, 32 & 33
WEEK 8	Sessions 10, 11 & 12		WEEK 23	Sessions 34, 35 & 36
WEEK 9	Sessions 13, 14 & 15		WEEK 24	Sessions 34, 35 & 36
WEEK 10	Sessions 13, 14 & 15		WEEK 25	Sessions 37, 38 & 39
WEEK 11	Sessions 16, 17 & 18		WEEK 26	Sessions 37, 38 & 39
WEEK 12	Sessions 16, 17 & 18		WEEK 27	Sessions 40, 41 & 42
WEEK 13	Sessions 19, 20 & 21		WEEK 28	Sessions 40, 41 & 42
WEEK 14	Sessions 19, 20 & 21		WEEK 29	Sessions 43, 44 & 45
WEEK 15	Sessions 22, 23 & 24		WEEK 30	Sessions 43, 44 & 45

Practice Format

Each practice in the sessions includes clear diagrams with supporting training notes:

- Session Objective
- Name of Practice
- Description
- Variations/Progressions (if applicable)
- Coaching Points

Key

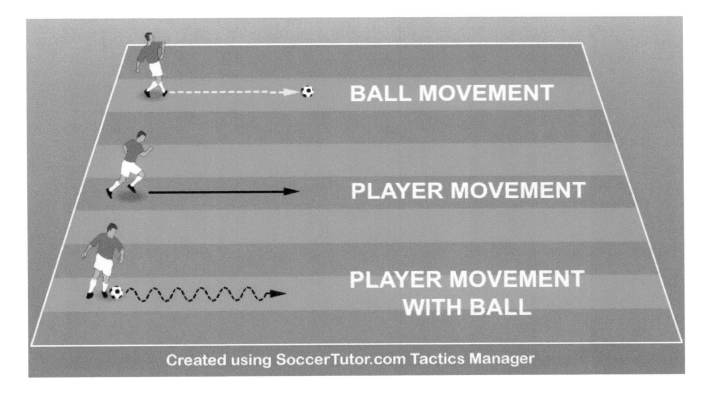

BALL MOVEMENT

PLAYER MOVEMENT

PLAYER MOVEMENT WITH BALL

Created using SoccerTutor.com Tactics Manager

TRAINING UNIT FOR WEEK 1 & 2

Individual Tactical Objective: Frontal man marking, feints and dribbling.

Technical Objective: Running with the ball.

Motor Athletic Objective: Aerobic power.

Duration of Session: 105 minutes

We recommend starting the session with exercises for general mobility to prevent injuries.

1. Warm Up — Running with the Ball - 'Defensive Shadow' — 10 mins

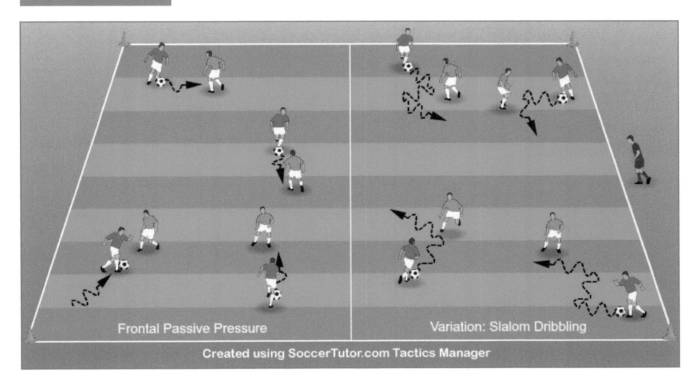

Frontal Passive Pressure

Variation: Slalom Dribbling

Created using SoccerTutor.com Tactics Manager

Description

Players are in pairs within a marked out area. One player with the ball is dribbling while another player is applying passive pressure from a frontal position. This is just passive pressure, testing the player's ability to keep the ball close to their feet.

The players change every minute.

Variations

1. Dribble in a slalom pattern (as shown on right side of diagram).
2. Introduce the concept of a strong side and a weak side.

Coaching Points

1. The players should constantly move the ball in the opposite direction to where the defender is.
2. Players should drop their shoulder when performing a feint or change of direction.

2. Conditioning | Interval Training 'Fartlek Running' | 15 mins

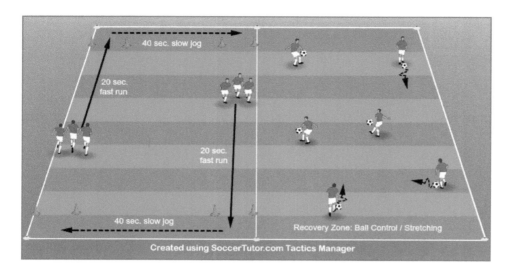

Description

5 minutes
Fartlek run
** - see below
40 seconds slow jog/ 20 seconds fast run.

2 minutes
Recovery

5 minutes
Fartlek
40 seconds slow jog/ 20 seconds fast run.

3 minutes
Stretching.

Coaching Points

1. Make sure the players keep moving for the slow jog part and do not stop.
2. The sprinting should be done at full intensity.

---

3. Technical | Dribbling with Feints / Moves to Beat | 20 mins

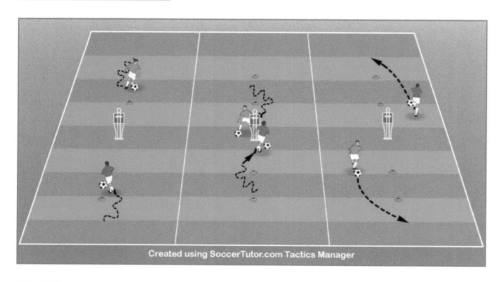

Description

2 players have a ball each and dribble through the cones (as shown).

When they reach the mannequin, they make a feint and move the ball to the right side and then continue running with the ball to the end of the line (switching places).

Variation

Use different feints (possibly specified by the coach).

Coaching Points

1. Players need to keep the ball close to their feet, so they can quickly change direction.
2. Use both feet and all parts of the foot for this practice, performing different dribbling techniques and feints/ moves to beat.

** Fartlek Running: A training technique, used especially among runners, consisting of bursts of intense effort (sprinting), alternating with less strenuous activity (jogging or walking).

4. Game Situation Frontal 1v1 Duel with Coloured Goals 20 mins

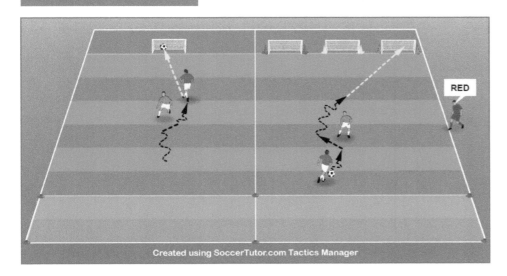

RED

Description

SITUATION A
The attacker tries to score in the goal. If the defender wins the ball they try to dribble into the end zone to score.

SITUATION B
Each goal is assigned a colour. The coach will call out the colour of the goal the attacker must score in.

If the defender wins the ball, they try to dribble into the end zone to score.

Coaching Points

1. Encourage players to use feints/moves to beat in this 1v1 duel.
2. Strength and correct body shape is needed to prevent the defenders from winning the ball (getting your body in between the opponent and the ball).

5. Specific Game Man Marking 6 Goal Dribbling Game 20 mins

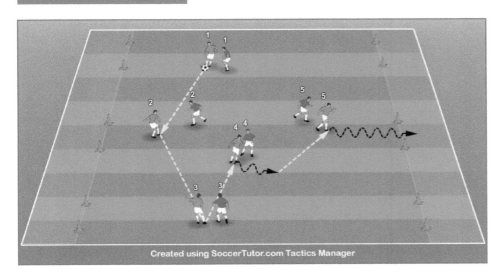

Description

We have a 5v5 game with 3 goals at each end.

Goals are scored by dribbling through the cone gates (goals).

Each player is assigned 1 opponent who they must mark. Players are not allowed to tackle any other player.

Coaching Points

1. Checking away before moving to receive is the key for creating space to receive when being man marked.
2. Use feints/moves to beat to take the ball past the defender.

Practice 6   Free Small Sided Game   20 mins

Individual Tactical Objective: Frontal man marking, feints and dribbling.

Technical Objective: Running with the ball.

Motor Athletic Objective: Strengthening and explosive power.

Duration of Session: 115 minutes

We recommend starting the session with exercises for general mobility to prevent injuries.

1. Warm Up   Running with the Ball and Dynamic Movements **20 mins**

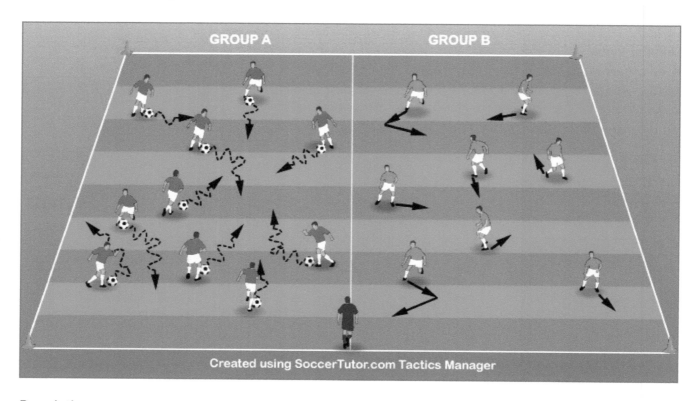

Description

GROUP A

Dribbling with a ball in traffic with general mobility and stretching.

GROUP B

In this area we work on coordination. This includes various types of running, focusing on running backwards and in a slalom pattern. We also imitate the typical run of a player marking or jockeying.

Variation

Change the type of dribbling every 2 minutes.

Coaching Point

1. The players with the ball need to have good awareness to avoid collisions and soft touches to keep close control of the ball in tight areas.

2. Conditioning — Strengthening and Speed Power

15 mins

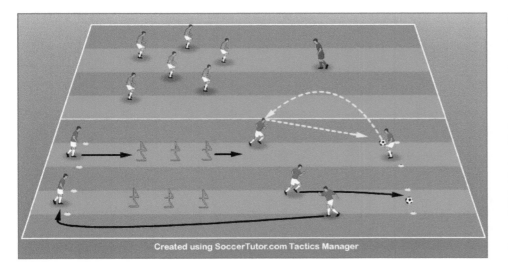

Created using SoccerTutor.com Tactics Manager

Description

3 minutes
15 Squats
(Maintain the position for 10 seconds, recovery for 10 seconds).

2 minutes
Stretching.

3 minutes
Squat jump (Maintain the position for 10 seconds, jump and recovery for 10 seconds).

6 minutes
In pairs, jump over 3 hurdles and then head the ball back from a teammate's throw (as shown).

Coaching Point

1. Monitor the players in this exercise to ensure all aspects are performed at a high intensity.

3. Technical — Changing Direction Team Shooting Game

15-20 mins

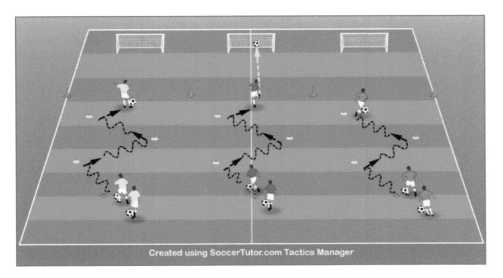

Created using SoccerTutor.com Tactics Manager

Description

Players are divided into 3 teams. A player from each team starts by dribbling to one cone and performs a predetermined feint, then dribbles to the next cone and performs another feint.

The player finishes by shooting in the small goal. The team that scores the most goals in a set time wins.

Coaching Points

1. When running with the ball and changing direction the players need to decelerate using short steps and bend the knees before accelerating in the opposite direction.

2. Although the players have to dribble the ball very quickly in this race, they need to still focus on accuracy through the cones using soft touches.

4. Game Situation   Quick Reactions and Finishing in a 1v2 Frontal Marking Duel

20 mins

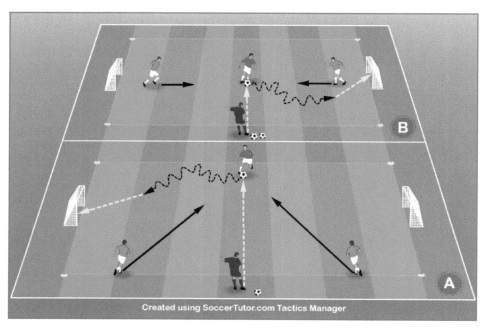

Created using SoccerTutor.com Tactics Manager

Description

SITUATION A
The coach passes the ball to the attacker who attacks one of the goals.

2 defenders apply pressure as soon as the ball is passed.

SITUATION B
The same situation as A but the defenders start from different positions, as shown in the diagram.

Coaching Points

1. The attacker needs to take a good directional first touch to get in a position to shoot as early as possible.

2. Encourage players to use feints/moves to beat to attack the space in behind the defender and score.

5. Specific Game   7v7 Position Specific Zonal Game

20 mins

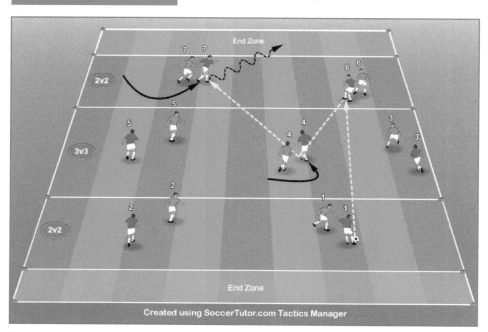

Created using SoccerTutor.com Tactics Manager

Description

The pitch is divided into 5 zones. We have 2v2s in the attacking zones and a 3v3 in the midfield zone.

Players only mark their assigned man (numbered).

Goals are scored by first passing through all the zones and then dribbling through the end zone.

If a defender passes to an attacker the next pass must go back to a midfielder (middle zone).

If an attacker wins the ball in the attacking zone, he must pass back to a midfielder. If a midfielder wins the ball, they must pass back to a defender.

Practice 6   Free Small Sided Game

20 mins

SESSION 03

Individual Tactical Objective: Frontal man marking and crossing.

Group Tactical Objective: Shifting and using width.

Technical Objective: Running with the ball.

Motor Athletic Objective: Quickness.

Duration of Session: 105 minutes

We recommend starting the session with exercises for general mobility to prevent injuries.

---

1. Warm Up   Quick Reactions in a Man Marking Dribbling Game   **15 mins**

Created using SoccerTutor.com Tactics Manager

Description

Players are divided into 2 teams, with 1 attacking team and 1 defending team. Every player starts the drill with a ball as they all dribble the ball around the area avoiding each other. We also have 6 different cone gates (goals) positioned on the sides of the area.

On the coach's whistle (or visual as shown in the diagram), the attacking players try to score by dribbling through the small goals. The defending players leave their ball to defend and tackle the attacking players.

Players are put into pairs and assigned 1 player to mark. They are not allowed to tackle the other players.

Variation

Change the type of dribbling

Coaching Points

1. Quick reactions are essential to get in front of the defender and score quickly.
2. The correct body shape is required to shield the ball, making sure their body is a barrier between the opponent and the ball.

2. Conditioning Quickness Circuit

15 mins

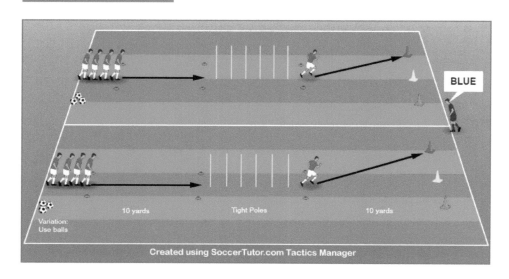

Description

7 Minutes
At first the players sprint 10 yards, then run through the poles and finally sprint the last 10 yards towards a coloured cone (called out by the coach). Players perform 10 repetitions

3 minutes
Stretching.

5 minutes
Juggling and volley passes in pairs under condition of quickness.

3. Technical Dribbling with Frontal Marking in 1v1 Channels

20 mins

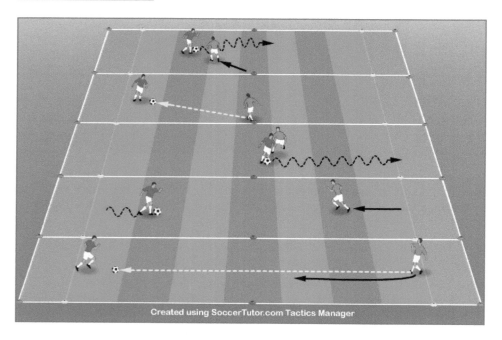

Description

Divide the playing area into mini zones as shown in the diagram.

The first player passes the ball and then moves to apply passive pressure. The player with the ball dribbles forwards and plays a 1v1 situation with the defender who moves backwards until the attacker reaches the opposite end.

Ask the players to change position so the angle of the defender's approach changes (as shown in the top 2 zones).

Coaching Point

1. Attackers need to maintain very close control of the ball when under pressure of frontal marking, also making sure to always keep the ball moving.

4. Game Situation — Back 4 Closing Down and 1v1 Duels   20 mins

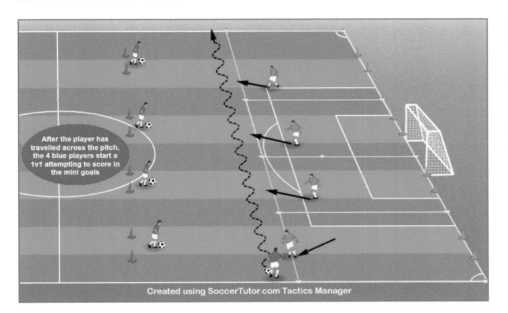

After the player has travelled across the pitch, the 4 blue players start a 1v1 attempting to score in the mini goals

Created using SoccerTutor.com Tactics Manager

Description

We start with 4 defenders located in the 4 zones as shown in the diagram.

1 player with the ball runs across the pitch and the defenders perform the correct movement to close down the bal carrier when he approaches their zone.

Once the player has travelled across the pitch, all 4 of the other players dribble forward to each start a 1v1 with one of the 4 defenders, all trying to score in the mini goals

Coaching Points

1. The cohesive movement in the first part should be monitored to ensure it is correct.
2. The defenders should apply immediate pressure on the ball carriers.

---

5. Specific Game — 1v1 Side Zones in an 8v8 Small Sided Game   20 mins

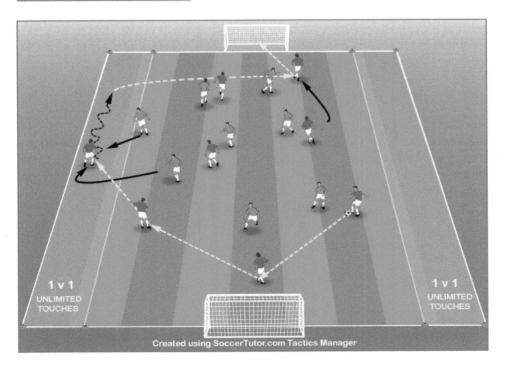

1 v 1
UNLIMITED
TOUCHES

1 v 1
UNLIMITED
TOUCHES

Created using SoccerTutor.com Tactics Manager

Description

We play a game with 2 side zones. The players play with 2 touches in the middle and have unlimited touches in the side zones.

1 player from the team in possession can move into the side zone and if they receive the ball, 1 player from the opposing team can enter that zone to defend.

If the attacking player wins the 1v1, they can cross without anymore pressure from the defender (unless he moves out of the channel and another player moves into it).

Practice 6   Free Small Sided Game   20 mins

TRAINING UNIT FOR WEEK 3 & 4

Individual Tactical Objective: Man marking from behind.

Technical Objective: Running with the ball.

Motor Athletic Objective: Aerobic power.

Duration of Session: 120 minutes

We recommend starting the session with exercises for general mobility to prevent injuries.

| 1. Warm Up | One Touch Play with One-Two Combinations | 15 mins |

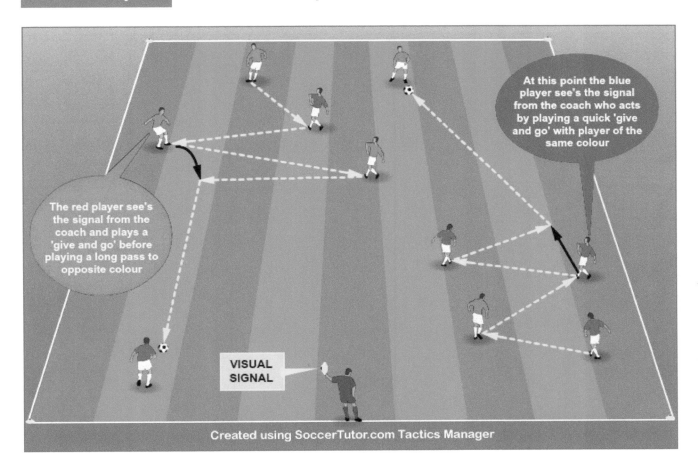

At this point the blue player see's the signal from the coach who acts by playing a quick 'give and go' with player of the same colour

The red player see's the signal from the coach and plays a 'give and go' before playing a long pass to opposite colour

VISUAL SIGNAL

Created using SoccerTutor.com Tactics Manager

Description

In a marked out area, the players pass the ball with 1 touch to a player of a different colour.

When the coach raises a cone with their arm (visual signal), the player in possession of the ball plays a 1-2 combination with a player of the same colour and then plays a long pass to a player of a different colour.

Coaching Points

1. There needs to be a focus on weight of the passes as the players perform both short and long passes.
2. With 1-2 combinations, the second pass needs to be out in front of the player to make the next pass with 1 touch.

2. Conditioning — Interval Training 'Fartlek Running' (2)   20 mins

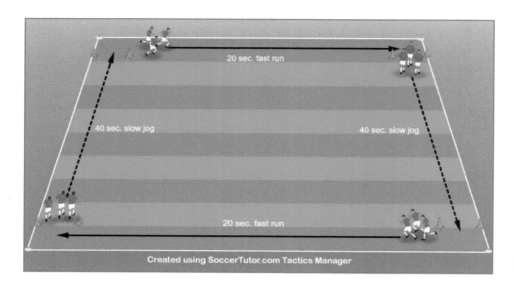

Description

5 minutes
Fartlek run:
** - see below

40 seconds slow jog/
20 seconds fast run.

3 minutes
Recovery.

7 minutes
Fartlek run:
40 seconds slow jog/
20 seconds fast run.

3 minutes
Stretching.

3. Technical — Dribbling with Different Obstacles   15-20 mins

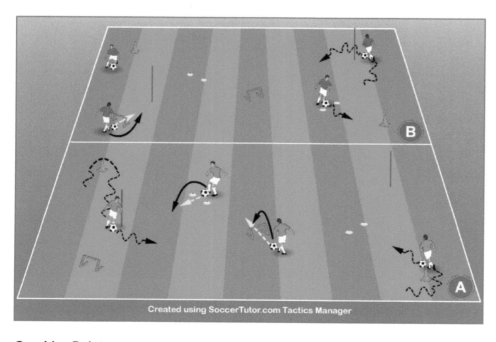

Description

In a marked out area we place various objects (cones, poles, hurdles etc) in a square.

Players dribble the ball and work around the obstacles, first without conditions, then based on the coach's command:

1. Using only the inside/ outside of the feet.

2. Using only the left or right foot.

3. Juggling the ball.

Coaching Points

1. Awareness is key to perform different techniques with the various obstacles and avoid collisions.

2. Players should use soft touches, keeping close control of the ball.

** Fartlek Running: A training technique, used especially among runners, consisting of bursts of intense effort (sprinting), alternating with less strenuous activity (jogging or walking).

4. Game Situation — Receiving a Ball on the Ground with Close Marking from Behind

20 mins

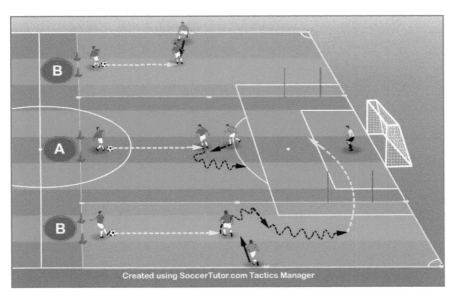

Created using SoccerTutor.com Tactics Manager

Description

We have 3 zones with players receiving passes in 1v1 situations.

In zone A, the defender marks the attacker from behind, trying to force the attacker onto their weaker foot.

In the B zones, the defenders are positioned to the side and must try to force the attacker towards the centre and

In zone A, the objective of the attacker is to score in the goal. In the B zones, the objective is to cross the ball through the 2 poles as shown in the picture. The defenders starting position is right behind the attacker.

---

5. Specific Game — Target Players and Close Marking from Behind in a 3 Zone Small Sided Game

30 mins

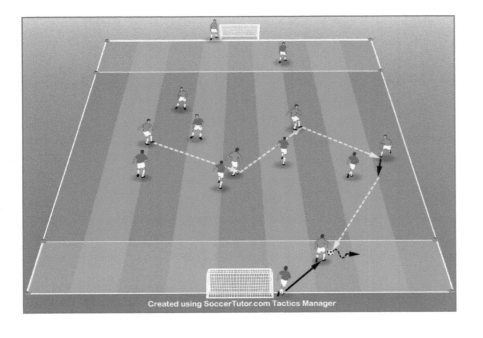

Created using SoccerTutor.com Tactics Manager

Description

We play a 5v5 game with 1 target player and a defender at each end.

The objective is to pass the ball to the target player to score.

A defender stands beside each goal and every time the ball is played to the target player, he must apply pressure and prevent the target player from turning towards the goal and scoring.

Practice 6   Free Small Sided Game

20 mins

Individual Tactical Objective: Man marking from behind.

Technical Objective: Running with the ball and shooting.

Motor Athletic Objective: Strengthening and explosive power.

Duration of Session: 115 minutes

We recommend starting the session with exercises for general mobility to prevent injuries.

1. Warm Up — Possession and Long Passing Transition Game — 20 mins

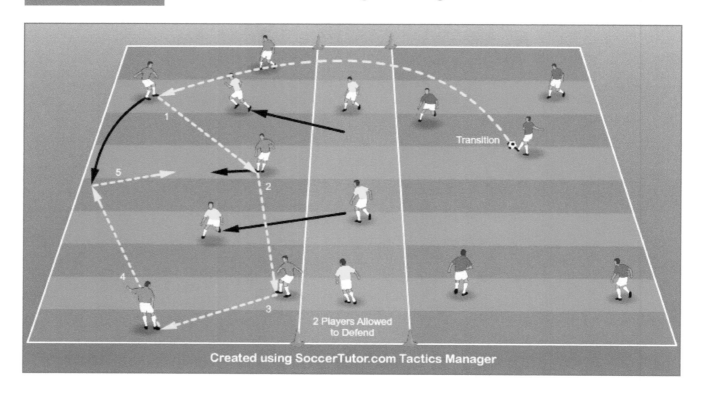

Transition

2 Players Allowed to Defend

Created using SoccerTutor.com Tactics Manager

Description

We have 3 teams of 5 players. Divide the area into 3 zones as shown in the diagram.

The team in possession (blue) play a long pass to the team in red. This team must make 5 passes before making a long pass back to the blue team.

The yellow team must use 2 players to apply pressure in the appropriate zone, but 3 players must remain in the middle zone trying to intercept the ball.

If the defending team win the ball, they must pass the ball to the other team and the team who lost possession must then apply pressure (becoming the defending team).

Full warm up schedule:

1. Transition Game - 4 minutes.

2. Dynamic Stretching - 5 minutes.

3. Transition Game - 4 minutes.

4. Dynamic Stretching - 5 minutes.

2. Conditioning — Strengthening and Explosive Power — 15 mins

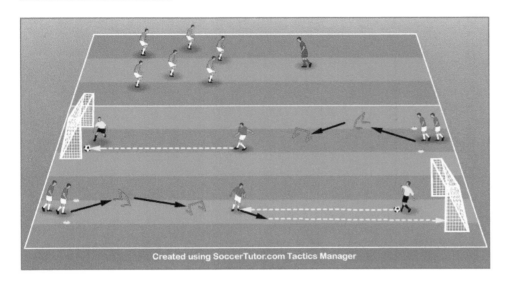

Description

4 minutes
20 Squats (Maintain position for 10 seconds and recover for 10 seconds).

2 minutes
Stretching.

4 minutes
20 squats (Maintain position for 10 seconds, jump and recover for 10 seconds).

5 minutes
The players jump over the 2 hurdles, receive the ball from the goalkeeper and shoot.

3. Technical — Receiving, Turning and Dribbling with the Back to Goal — 15-20 mins

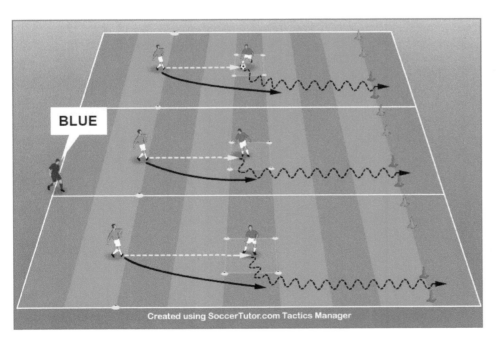

BLUE

Description

Players stand in the yellow square zones as shown in the diagram.

They receive a pass from their teammate, turn and dribble towards the coloured goal called out by the coach.

They must dribble through the cone goal while the teammate who passed the ball applies pressure from behind.

Coaching Points

1. The player should receive the ball on the half turn to make a quick transition to dribble the ball towards the cones.
2. A directional first touch is very important to quickly move towards the cone before the defender is able to close them down.

4. Game Situation   2v1 / 2v2 Man Marking from Behind   20 mins

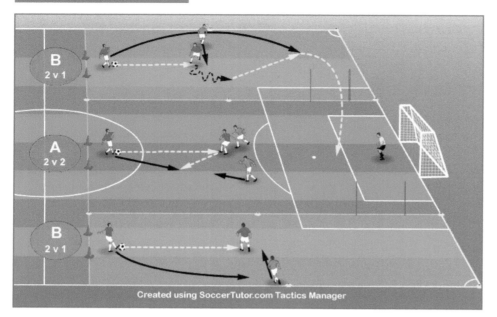

Created using SoccerTutor.com Tactics Manager

Description

We have 3 zones with players receiving passes.

In zone A, there are 2 defenders and 1 of them marks the attacker from behind. The passer makes it a 2v2 situation.

In the B zones, the defenders are positioned to the side and must try to prevent the attacker from turning towards the poles and crossing the ball.

In zone A, the objective is to score in the goal. In the B zones, the objective is to cross the ball through the 2 poles as shown in the diagram.

Variation

Defenders start from a distance of 4 yards away from the attacker (much nearer).

5. Specific Game   1v1 Man Marking in a 7 Zone Game   20 mins

Created using SoccerTutor.com Tactics Manager

Description

The area is divided into 1 central zone and 6 smaller zones.

1 attacker and 1 defender are in each small zone and the attackers have their backs to goal. After 4 passes in the central zone the ball can be passed to any of the attackers.

If the attacker beats the defender, they can shoot in the goal

Variation

1 midfielder can move into one of the zones to create a 2v1 against the 1 defender.

Practice 6   Free Small Sided Game   20 mins

Individual Tactical Objective: Man marking from behind and passing on the ground.

Group Tactical Objective: Defensive movement and support play.

Technical Objective: Running with the ball.

Motor Athletic Objective: Psycho-kinetics and quickness.

Duration of Session: 110 minutes

We recommend starting the session with exercises for general mobility to prevent injuries.

| **1. Warm Up** | Defensive Support Play Practice | **15 mins** |

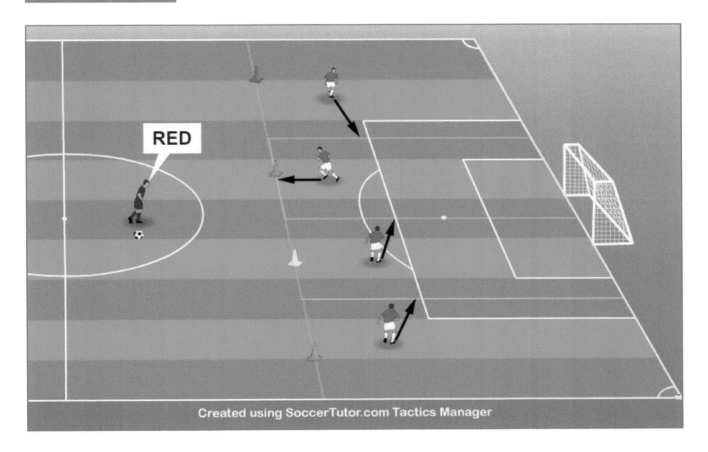

Created using SoccerTutor.com Tactics Manager

Description

This is a tactical exercise for the defensive unit focusing on providing support.

The coach calls out a colour and the player standing in the zone of the same colour must quickly close down the space, while the other players move to provide cover in behind.

This practice works with a back 4 which can be applied for a 4-4-2, 4-3-3, 4-2-3-1 etc.

Coaching Points

1. The timing and cohesion of the movements needs to be closely monitored.
2. Even though 1 defender has moved forwards, the other 3 should still be in a straight line behind.

2. Conditioning — Technical Quickness Circuit

15 mins

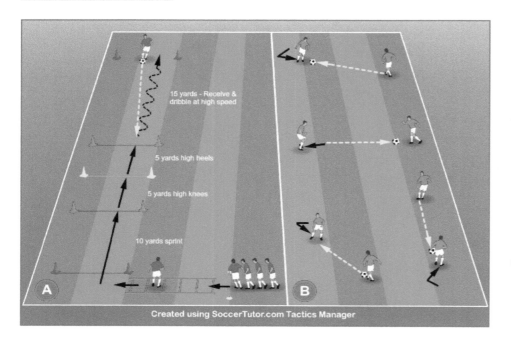

Description

7 minutes
Side-steps through the ladder, 10 yard sprint, 5 yards with high knees and 5 yards with high heels, then finally receiving the pass and running with the ball at high speed.

3 minutes
Stretching.

5 minutes
Passing and receiving in pairs under condition of quickness.

3. Technical — 1v1 with Frontal Marking / 1v1 with Back to Goal

20 mins

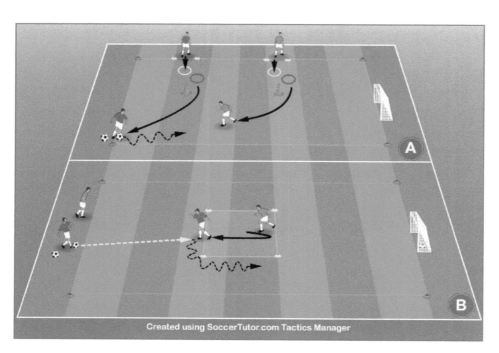

Description

SITUATION A
We have a coordination exercise, hopping through the rings and running round the cone. The blue player runs to the ball and attacks. The red player runs to defend in a 1v1.

SITUATION B
Here we have a 1v1 with the players starting in a small square. The attacking player makes a movement to check away and receive the ball with his back to goal.

Coaching Points

1. Situation A: The player should use feints to beat the defender and attack the space in behind.
2. Situation B: A directional first touch and correct body shape for shielding is required in this 1v1.

4. Game Situation — Shifting of the Defensive Unit with a 4v4 — 20 mins

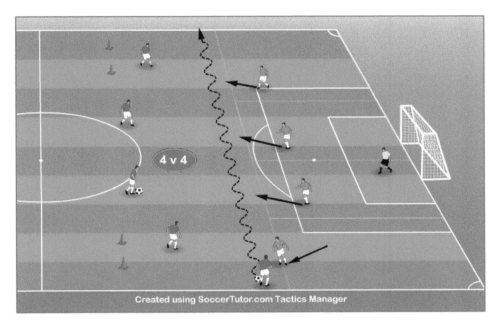

Created using SoccerTutor.com Tactics Manager

Description

1 player dribbles across the pitch in front of the back 4.

The defenders work on closing down and providing support to each other in relation to where the ball is.

When the player has dribbled the ball to the other side, 4 attacking players will start a 4v4 against the defenders.

The aim is to score in the goal.

Variation

Add 2 cone gates (goals) for the defenders to score in if they win the ball, as shown in the diagram.

5. Specific Game — Awareness in a '2 Teams, 4 Colours Game' — 20 mins

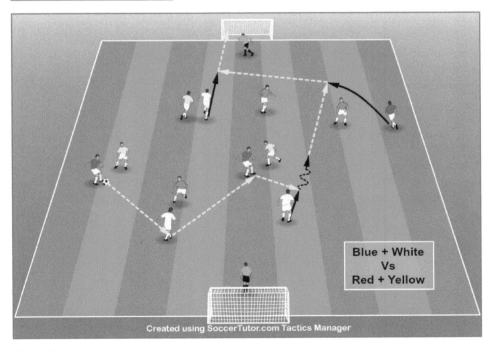

Blue + White
Vs
Red + Yellow

Created using SoccerTutor.com Tactics Manager

Description

We play a 7v7 game with each team made up of 2 colours with the condition that the players cannot pass the ball to a teammate with the same colour.

The aim is to build up play and score as normal.

Variations

1. Play with the hands.
2. One colour per team plays with limited touches

Coaching Points

1. Correct body shape (open up on the half turn) and positioning is important to view where the next pass goes.
2. Good communication, movement and vision are essential with limited passing options.

Practice 6 — Free Small Sided Game — 20 mins

TRAINING UNIT FOR WEEK 5 & 6

Individual Tactical Objective: Man marking from behind with the ball passed in the air and creating space.

Technical Objective: Running with the ball and shooting.

Motor Athletic Objective: Aerobic power.

Duration of Session: 110 minutes

We recommend starting the session with exercises for general mobility to prevent injuries.

1. Warm Up Switching Play with Support Players in End Zones   15 mins

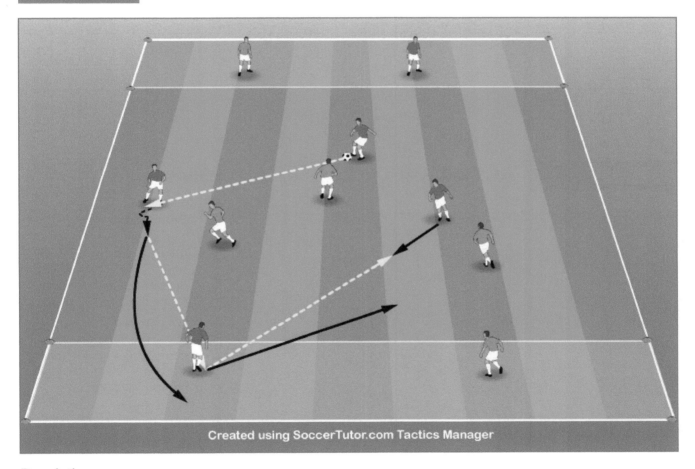

Created using SoccerTutor.com Tactics Manager

Description

Each team has 5 players, 3 in the central playing area and 1 player in each end zone.

A point is scored each time the ball is passed from one side to the other. The aim is to switch the play.

The player that passes to the outside must trade places with the outside player.

Coaching Points

1. When the players are exchanging positions in the end zones, they need to do so quickly and provide a passing option to keep possession.

2. Correct body shape (open up on the half-turn) and positioning is important to view the options for where the next pass is going.

2. Conditioning — Interval Training 'Fartlek Running' (3)   15 mins

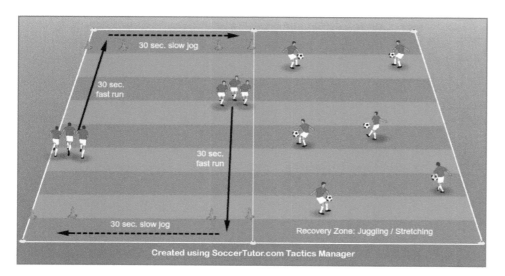

Description

10 minutes
Fartlek run (30 seconds slow jog and 30 seconds sprinting).

2 minutes
Active recovery with juggling.

3 minutes
Stretching.

---

3. Technical — Running with the Ball, Feints and Shooting   20 mins

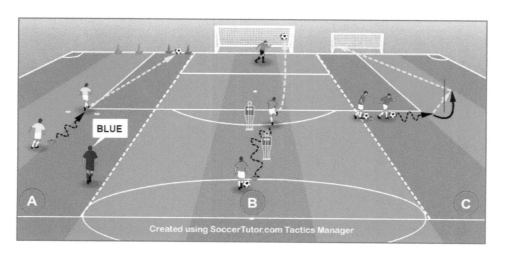

Description

SITUATION A
Running with the ball and shooting into the goal with the same colour called out by the coach.

SITUATION B
Players run with the ball performing a feint to the left then a feint to the right, followed by a shot.

SITUATION C
Players run with the ball, pass around the pole, run around it and shoot first time.

Coaching Points

1. Players need to keep close control of the ball for all aspects of this exercise.
2. The accuracy of the shot is important, and not the power.

4. Game Situation — 1v1 Back to Goal Duel with Goalkeepers — 20 mins

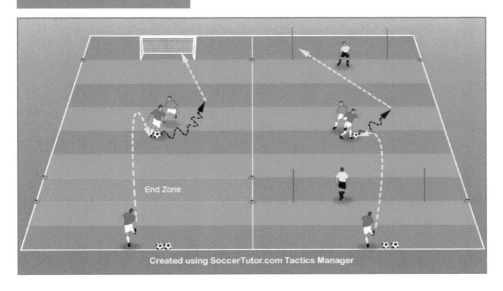

Description

In the first part we have a 1v1 with the attacking player receiving a high ball with his back to goal and the aim to score in the small goal. If the defender wins the ball, he must dribble through the end zone to get a point.

In the second part we have a 1v1 with 2 goals and 2 goalkeepers.

We have the same practice as in A, but this time if the defender wins the ball he must shoot in the other goal.

Coaching Points

1. Players need to check away before moving to receive the pass.
2. When receiving a high pass, the player needs to put their body in between the defender and the ball.

5. Specific Game — 1v1 Duels in a 5 Zone Game — 20 mins

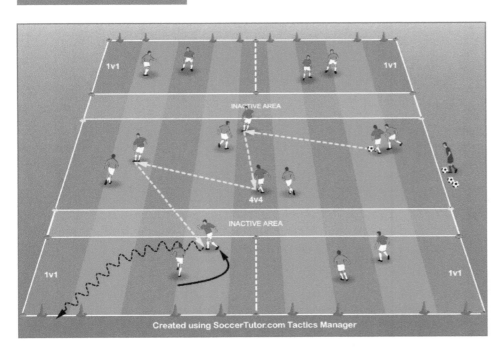

Description

We have 5 zones and there is a 4v4 situation in the central zone. After 3 passes the team in possession of the ball must make a long pass to one of the attacking players in the end zones who play a 1v1 against a defender.

The attacking player must dribble through one of the small goals. If the defender wins the ball, he will make a long pass to a teammate and the pass cannot be intercepted.

Change the positions of the players often.

Practice 6   Free Small Sided Game — 20 mins

Individual Tactical Objective: Man marking from behind, passing in the air and changes of direction.

Technical Objective: Running with the ball and long passing in the air.

Motor Athletic Objective: Explosive power.

Duration of Session: 110 minutes

We recommend starting the session with exercises for general mobility to prevent injuries.

| **1. Warm Up** | RWTB, Volley Passing & Juggling with the Weaker Foot | **15 mins** |

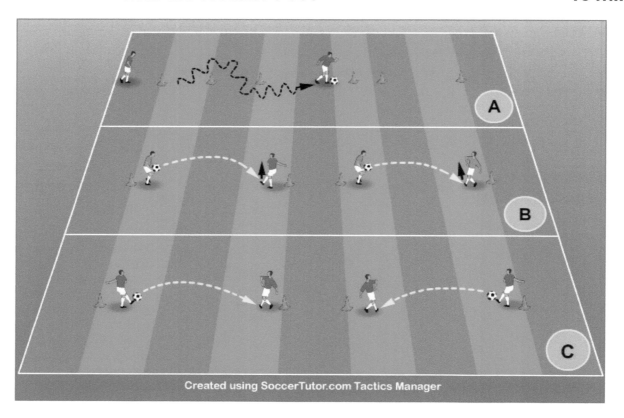

Created using SoccerTutor.com Tactics Manager

Description

Here we have 3 stations working on their weaker foot, with players having 5 minutes in each station.

A) Dribble around cones with the weaker foot. Place the cones at varying distances (change throughout).

B) Players juggle and after 3 touches pass to their teammate who receives the ball with their weaker foot. Change method of receiving the ball every minute; inside of foot, outside of foot, instep, sole.

C) In pairs, players pass and receive with their weaker foot. Variations are a volley with the instep, volley with the inside of the foot, half volley & chest control and volley back.

Coaching Points

1. Monitor the correct technique for receiving and passing the ball in the air.

2. Make sure players use all the different parts of their foot to volley pass in this exercise.

2. Conditioning — Explosive Power Training Circuit

15 mins

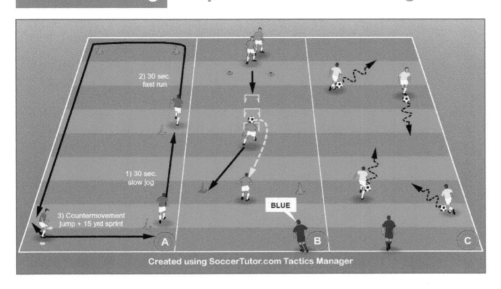

Description

Here we have an explosive power training circuit, with 3 sections which last 5 minutes each.

A) Counter-movement jump + 15 yard sprint.

Fartlek run which is 30 seconds slow jog and 30 seconds fast run.

2 minutes:
Stretching

B) Jump over 3 hurdles, head the ball and sprint to the cone with the colour called out by the coach.

C) 5 yard sprints with the ball.

---

3. Technical — RWTB and Turning / Changing Direction

20 mins

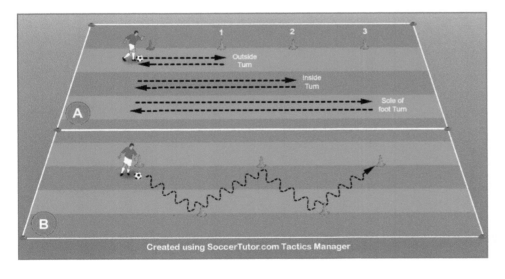

Description

PART A
180 degrees changes of direction. The players run with the ball back and forth as shown in the diagram. Set up 3 cones 5 yards apart.

Start dribbling, turn with the outside of the foot on the first cone, with the inside of the foot on the second cone and turn with the sole of the foot on the third cone.

PART B
Diagonal changes of direction from one cone to the next.

Coaching Points

1. We want quick and sharp changes of direction.
2. The correct technique and body shape should be used for the different types of turn (outside, inside and sole).

4. Game Situation — Receiving the Ball in 1v1 Situations in and Around the Penalty Area

20 mins

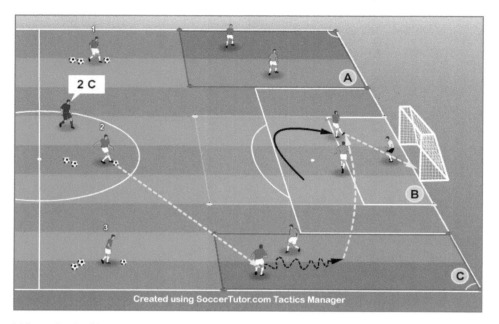

Description

In this practice, we have 3 zones (A, B & C as shown in the diagram). In zone B, there is 1 forward vs 1 centre back, in the other 2 zones (A & C) there is 1 winger vs 1 full back.

Outside these zones, we have 3 midfield players all with a ball numbered 1-3. These players wait for the coach to call out their number and which zone they should pass the ball into. In the diagram, player 2 passes into zone C for the winger to receive and play a 1v1 vs the defender.

When the ball is passed into zone B, the striker has to shoot on goal. When the ball arrives in zones A & C, the winger has to cross for the forward to finish in zone B where there is a 1v1 situation against the centre back.

5. Specific Game — 4v4 with 4 Goals in a Small Sided Game

20 mins

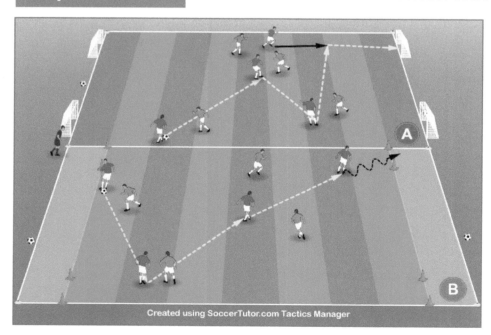

Description

PITCH A
4v4 game with 4 mini goals (2 at each end). The players use a maximum of 3 touches.

PITCH B
4v4 game with 4 cone gate goals.

The players must dribble through the cones to score and can again only use a minimum of 3 touches.

Coaching Points

1. There should be a mixture of passes to feet and passes into space.
2. The players need quick movements to dominate the 1v1 situations and dribble through the cones.

Practice 6 Free Small Sided Game

20 mins

SESSION 09

Individual Tactical Objective: Man marking from behind and aerial passing.

Group Tactical Objective: Defensive movements (diagonal) and covering.

Technical Objective: Running with the ball and long passing in the air.

Motor Athletic Objective: Quickness.

Duration of Session: 110 minutes

We recommend starting the session with exercises for general mobility to prevent injuries.

---

1. Warm Up 4 Colours, 2 Team Game   15 mins

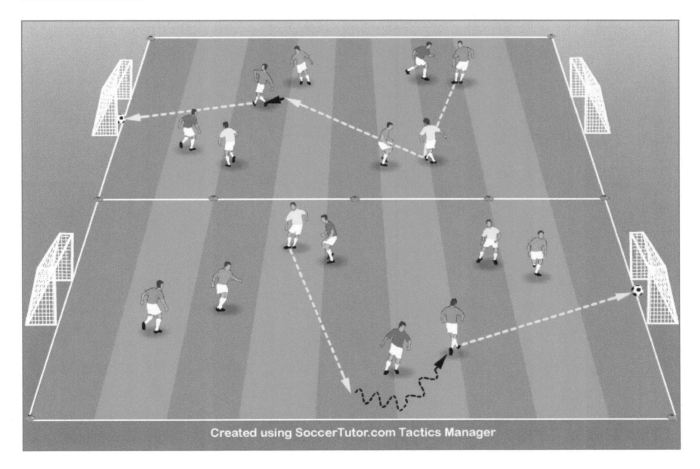

Created using SoccerTutor.com Tactics Manager

Description

In an area 20 x 20 yards, we play a 4v4 small sided game with each team made up of 2 colours. In the diagram the reds are playing with the yellows and the blues are playing with the oranges.

One colour plays with limited touches (1,2 or 3) and the other colour plays with unlimited touches.

Coaching Points

1. Correct body shape (open up on the half turn) and positioning is important to view where the next pass goes.

2. Good communication, movement and vision are essential with limited passing options.

2. Conditioning — Quickness Circuit with Turning — 10 mins

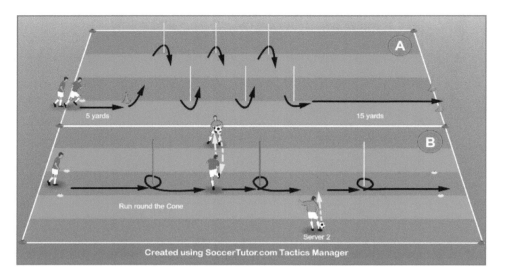

Description

PART A
Low skip for 5 yards + diagonal running around the 6 poles as shown + 15 yard sprint to finish (all without the ball).

PART B
Sprint, perform a full 360 turn around the pole + volley pass the ball served by a teammate.

Repeat with normal pass, turn round the last cone and sprint to the end.

Work for 5 minutes on each part.

3. Technical — Ball Control, Crossing and Finishing Practice — 20 mins

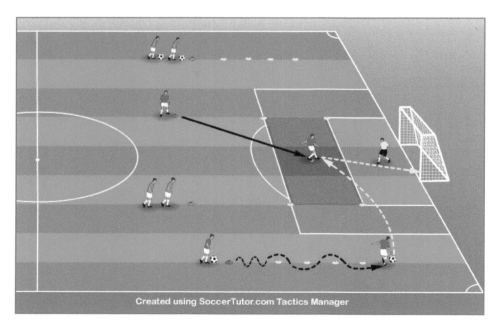

Description

The wide players start on the flank with a ball each and must dribble around the cones and cross into the box.

At the edge of the penalty area, another group of players must make a diagonal run to receive the cross and shoot in the goal past the goalkeeper.

Run the drill from both sides.

Coaching Point

1. The pass and the run need to be timed well together to prevent the player having to slow down or halt their run before shooting at goal.

4. Game Situation Man Marking in the Penalty Area from Crosses on the Flank

25 mins

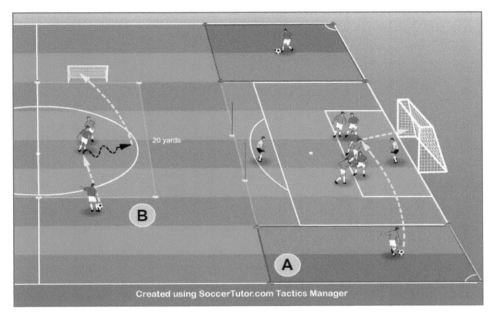

Description

EXERCISE A

Here we practice man marking on crosses from a standing position.

Inside the penalty area, there are 3 pairs of players each of whom is assigned a player they are marking.

The wingers cross 5 times each and the players in the box must defend and attack. After 10 crosses rotate the player's roles.

EXERCISE B

1v1 with attacking player who has his back to goal. The defender can anticipate the attacker. If the defender wins the ball he can get a point if he passes the ball to his teammate's chest. When the attacker loses possession he must prevent the the defender from passing to his teammate.

---

5. Specific Game Wide Play, Crossing & Defensive Covering with a 2v2 in the Penalty Area

20 mins

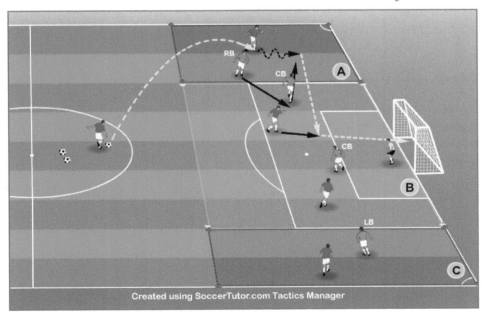

Description

The coach plays a long pass into zone A or B where the defender starts from a higher position than the winger.

The centre back must close down the winger and the full back must trade places with the centre back as shown in the diagram.

The winger and the centre back have a 1v1 situation with the objective for the winger cross into the central zone where a 2v2 is played.

The other players will play a 5v5 game with a maximum of 2 touches.

After 10 minutes, the players switch stations.

Practice 6 Free Small Sided Game	**20 mins**

TRAINING UNIT FOR WEEK 7 & 8

Individual Tactical Objective: Feints, dribbling and man marking.

Technical Objective: Running with the ball.

Motor Athletic Objective: Psycho-kinetics.

Duration of Session: 110 minutes

We recommend starting the session with exercises for general mobility to prevent injuries.

| **1. Warm Up** | 5v5 'Nutmeg' Possession Game | **15 mins** |

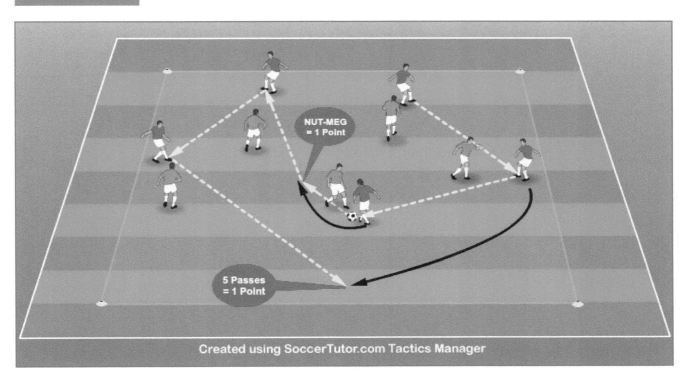

Created using SoccerTutor.com Tactics Manager

Description

In an area 20 x 20 yards we play a 5v5 game.

A team score 2 points if an opponent is beaten with a 'nutmeg' and the team maintain possession. A team can win 1 point if an opponent is beaten with a feint or normal dribbling and every time 5 passes are completed.

Play for 5 minutes, stretch for 2 minutes, play for 5 minutes and stretch for 2 minutes.

Coaching Points

1. The nutmeg needs to be weighted so that the player can receive the ball again without pressure.
2. Correct body shape (open up on the half turn) and positioning is important to view where the next pass is going.

2. Conditioning   Quick Reactions Colours Game   15 mins

Description

10 minutes
We have 4 teams all wearing different colours. 2 teams play against the other 2 teams.

Goals are scored in the goals with the colours of the opposition.

Change the alliances during the game to prompt quick reactions to a changing situation.

2 minutes
Active recovery juggling.

3 minutes
Stretching.

3. Technical   Dribbling at Speed with 'Nutmeg'   20 mins

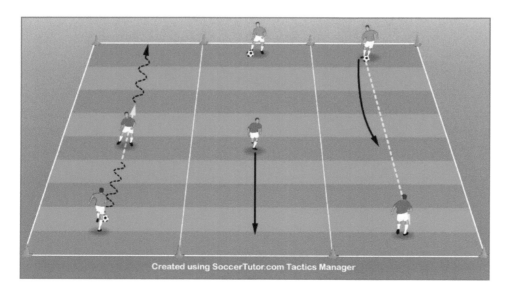

Description

The red player runs with the ball towards the blue player who is standing with his legs open.

The red player plays the ball through the blues' legs, collects the ball behind him and dribbles to the end.

The blue player sprints to the starting position to receive a pass from the red player.

The red player moves into the middle and the same sequence is then repeated with opposite roles.

Variations

1. The defender opens and closes his legs to make it harder for the attacker.
2. Dribble only with the right/left foot, inside/outside of foot, inside of both feet or only with the sole of the foot.

4. Game Situation   1v1 on the Flanks with Crossing & Finishing   20 mins

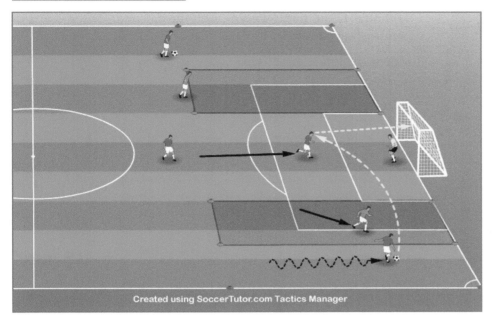

Created using SoccerTutor.com Tactics Manager

Description

The first player dribbles the ball forward on the flank with the aim to cross or to beat the defender and get into the box. An attacker waits in a centra position and times a run into the box to receive and score.

The defender is not allowed to leave the red zone. The defender scores a point every time he prevents the cross or stops the winger from dribbling into the penalty area.

Run the exercise from both sides of the pitch.

Coaching Points

1. Use a feint/move to beat to work the space for a cross.

2. The run needs to be timed well to meet the cross without stopping.

5. Specific Game   1v1 on the Flanks with Crossing & Finishing (2)   20 mins

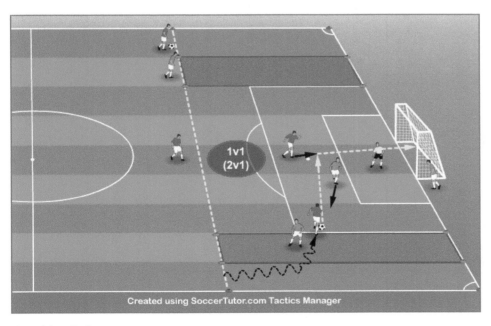

1v1
(2v1)

Created using SoccerTutor.com Tactics Manager

Description

The same situation as in the previous exercise is now progressed into a small game.

If the winger is successful with a cross, a 1v1 is played in the penalty area to attack/defend the ball.

If the winger dribbles round the defender a 2v2 situation is created inside the box.

Coaching Points

1. Awareness and good decision making is required to judge the right time to dribble into the box.

2. As the defender closes down the ball carrier in the 2v1, the other player should move easily into the space

| Practice 6   Free Small Sided Game | 20 mins |

Individual Tactical Objective: Marking a player standing on the opposite site in relation to the ball.

Technical Objective: Running with the ball and penetrating passes.

Motor Athletic Objective: Psycho-kinetics.

Duration of Session: 110 minutes

We recommend starting the session with exercises for general mobility to prevent injuries.

| **1. Warm Up** | *4v4 Rugby Game* | **15 mins** |

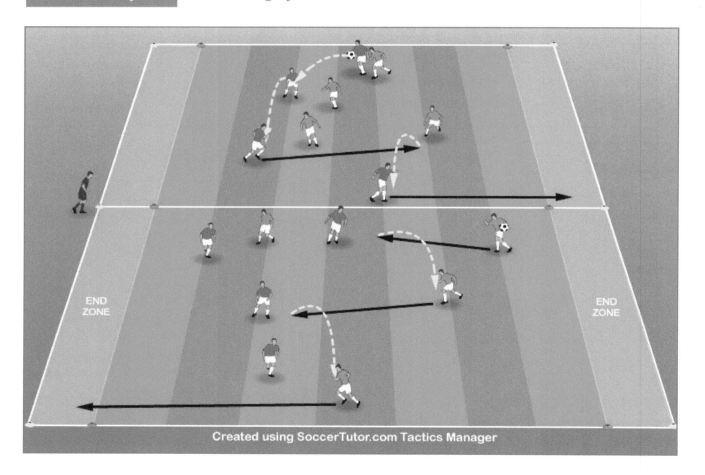

Description

In an area 30 x 20 yards we play a rugby style 4v4 game with a rugby ball (or football if you do not have one).

Goals are scored by running through the end zone. The ball can only be passed/thrown backwards.

Variations

1. Allow 1 forward pass.
2. Have the players kick the ball out of their hands to pass - volley or half volley.

2. Conditioning — Non Stop 6 Coloured Goals 3 Zone Possession Game

15 mins

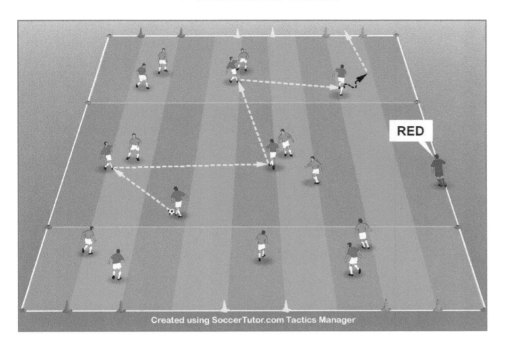

RED

Created using SoccerTutor.com Tactics Manager

Description

10 minutes
In the central zone we have a 3v3 and the aim is first to keep possession.

On the coach's call, the midfielders pass the ball to their forwards who play in a 3v2 in the end zone and must score in the goals with the colour called out by the coach. The game is played with no interruptions.

2 minutes
Recovery while juggling.

3 minutes
Stretching.

3. Technical — Running with the Ball and Penetrating Passes **20 mins**

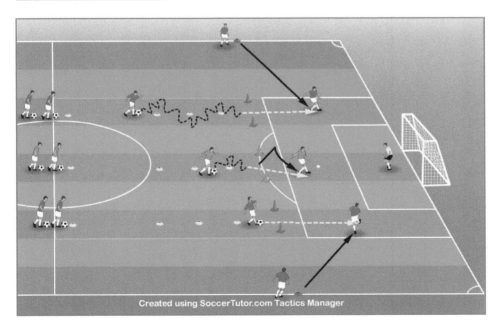

Created using SoccerTutor.com Tactics Manager

Description

The blue players who start with the ball dribble around the cones and then execute a penetrating pass towards the goal for the winger who makes a diagonal run from the touchline and shoots towards the far post.

In the centre, the red player's penetrating pass is for a central striker who must 'check away' before receiving the ball and shooting at goal.

Coaching Points

1. The central striker should check away and then receive on the half turn to make a quick transition to shoot.
2. Focus the attention on the technique, the body shape and positioning of the non striking foot for shooting.
3. Players should use different parts of their feet to shoot depending on the angle.

4. Game Situation — Creating Space to Receive Long Passes on the Flank

20 mins

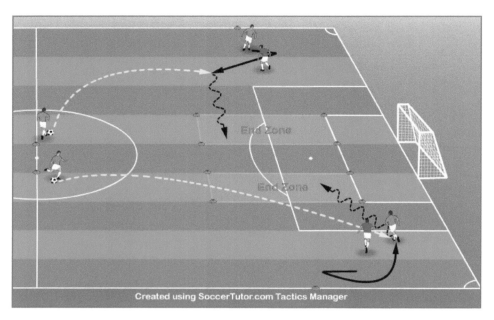

Created using SoccerTutor.com Tactics Manager

Description

2 players play long passes to the flank for their teammates.

The defender marks the attacker who makes either deep runs in behind or checks out and back in to receive the ball from the midfielder.

The attacking player must score by dribbling into the end zone. After 10 minutes switch sides.

Coaching Points

1. The pass needs to be accurate and timed well for the player to run onto and control.
2. The player receiving needs to check away from their marker with a quick, short movement before making a longer movement to receive in space.

5. Specific Game — Rugby Style 5v5 Small Sided Game

20 mins

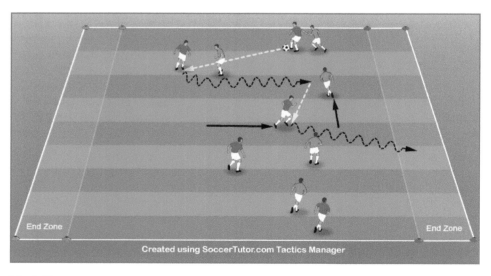

Created using SoccerTutor.com Tactics Manager

Description

In an area 30 x 20 yards we play a rugby style game.

Goals are scored by dribbling the ball through the end zone.

The ball can only be passed backwards.

Encourage the players to utilise 1v1 duels whenever possible.

Variations

1. Allow 1 forward pass.
2. If a goal is scored after a feint it is worth double.

Practice 6   Free Small Sided Game

20 mins

Individual Tactical Objective: Marking a player running from the opposite site in relation to the ball.

Group Tactical Objective: Support of the back 4 with the ball on the ground.

Technical Objective: Running with the ball and passing.

Motor Athletic Objective: Psycho-kinetics and quickness.

Duration of Session: 105 minutes

We recommend starting the session with exercises for general mobility to prevent injuries.

| 1. Warm Up | Passing and RWTB in Pairs | 15 mins |

Created using SoccerTutor.com Tactics Manager

Description

In an area 20 x 20 yards, the players are in pairs and pass the ball to each other under various conditions:

1. Passing after running with the ball.
2. Dribbling, feint and pass.
3. Dribbling and long pass with inside of the foot or the instep.
4. Throw and volley pass back with the inside of the foot.
5. Throw and volley pass back with the instep.
6. Throw and head the ball back.

Coaching Points

1. The pairs should maintain a distance of at least 5 yards at all times.
2. Make sure the players are proactive and keep the ball moving throughout this warm up.5. Throw and volley ass back with the instep. 6. Throw and head the ball back.

2. Conditioning Technical Quickness Circuit

10 mins

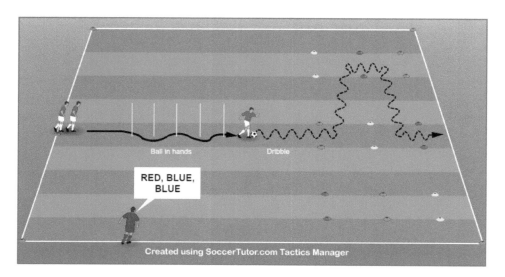

Description

7 minutes
Quick slalom running around the poles with ball in the hands.

The coach then calls a sequence of colours and the player will dribble through the cones following the same sequence called out by the coach.

3 minutes
In pairs the players perform technical exercises under condition of quickness (volley passes or juggling).

3. Technical Marking a Player Coming from the Opposite Side to the Ball

20 mins

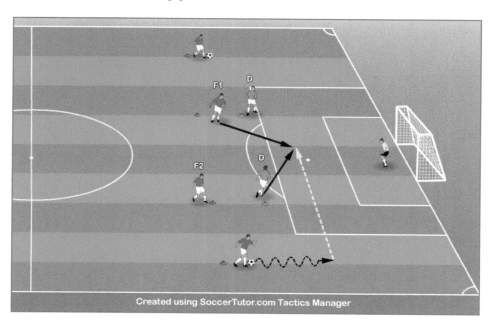

Description

The first player runs with the ball forwards along the side of the penalty area and passes the ball on the ground to F1 who makes a run from the opposite side.

The defender must move from his position in between the 2 attackers quickly to mark F1 and stop a shot on goal.

Variation

The ball is crossed after the player passes the ball to himself.

4. Game Situation — Back 4 Providing Support with the Ball on the Ground

20 mins

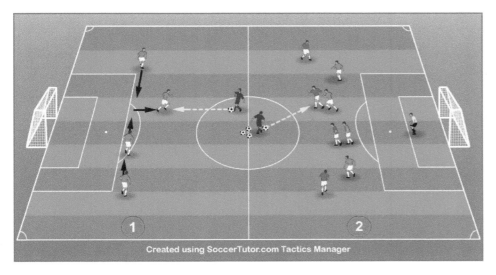

Description

EXERCISE 1

In the first 10 minutes the defenders practice the movements of support without the ball. The players will make the movements based on where the coach passes the ball.

With the ball on the flank, the coach will call whether to provide support with 2 or 3 lines.

The midfielders and forwards will work on their weak foot with dribbling exercises at this time.

EXERCISE 2

In the next 10 minutes we play a 4v4 game using half a pitch, with the defenders focusing on the movements they worked on in Exercise 1.‖

---

5. Specific Game — 4v4 with 4 Coloured Goals Possession Game

20 mins

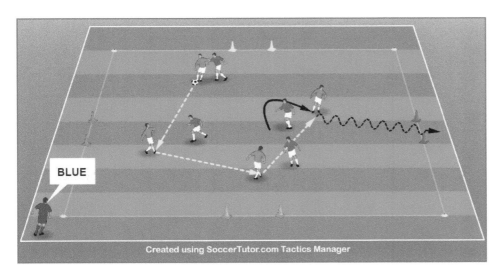

BLUE

Description

In an area 20 x 20 yards, we have 4 goals of different colours. We play a 4v4 with both teams trying to keep possession.

When the coach calls a colour, the player in possession of the ball can score by dribbling through the cones of that colour. (10 points) or by combination play (5 points)

Coaching Points

1. Players need to check away from their marker before moving to receive (creating space).

2. 1 touch passing should be used when possible to speed up play.

| Practice 6 | Free Small Sided Game | **20 mins** |

TRAINING UNIT FOR WEEK 9 & 10

Individual Tactical Objective: Marking and creating space.

Technical Objective: Diagonal passing.

Motor Athletic Objective: Specific work: Centre backs and forwards work on explosive power. Midfielders work on aerobic power and wide players work on acceleration and deceleration.

Duration of Session: 115 minutes

We recommend starting the session with exercises for general mobility to prevent injuries.

| 1. Warm Up | 5v5 Passing Gate Game | 20 mins |

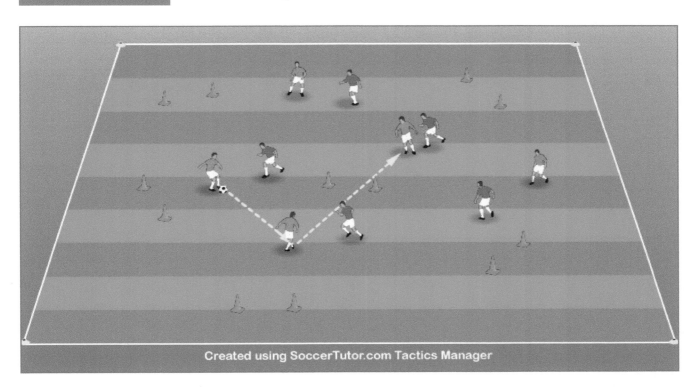

Created using SoccerTutor.com Tactics Manager

Description

In an area 30 x 20 yards, 2 teams of 5 players play a game trying to score by passing the ball through one of the small goals (cone gates). To score, the ball must be passed through the cones to a teammate, who must successfully control the ball.

Set out 1 goal more than the players in each team. In this example we have a 5v5, so have 6 goals.

Coaching Points

1. The timing of the movement with the pass is key to score 'goals' in this game.
2. Encourage players to mark 1 player each, aiming to prevent them passing or receiving the ball

2. Conditioning — Sprint Training & Quick Combinations — 20 mins

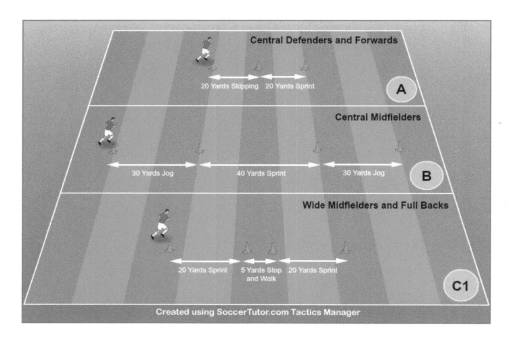

Description

Centre backs and Forwards
A) 20 yards skipping + 20 yard sprint with the ball.
(2 x 10 repetitions)

2 minutes:
Recovery.

5 minutes:
Heading in pairs.

Midfielders
B) 30 yard jog + 40 yard sprint + 30 yard (10 repetitions).

1 minute:
Recovery.

Full backs and Wide Midfielders
C1) 20 yard sprint, stop and walk 5 yards, 20 yard sprint. (2 x 10 repetitions).

2 minutes:
Recovery.

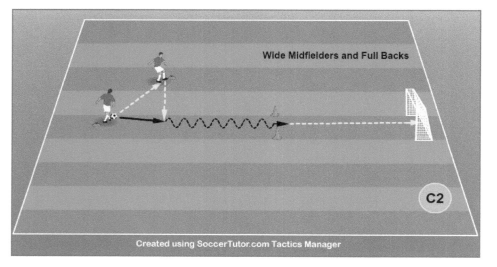

C2) The first player passes to their teammate, sprints to receive the ball from the 1-2, quickly dribbles through the cones and shoots in the small goal.

(5 minutes).

3. Technical — Diagonal Passing Square

15 mins

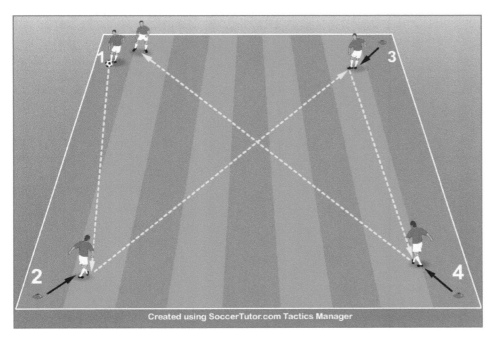

Description

5 players in a square pass the ball in a diagonal pattern as shown.

Player 1 plays a straight pass to Player 2, who plays a diagonal pass to 3. Player 3 plays a straight pass to 4 and Player 4 plays a diagonal pass to 5 and the sequence starts again.

Each player moves to the next position after their pass.

Variations

1. Change the direction of the passes.
2. One touch passing.

Coaching Points

1. Make sure the players communicate and heads are up.
2. Start the drill with 2 touches and quickly progress to 1 touch to speed up play.

4. Game Situation — Individual Tactics – Marking in a 1v1

20 mins

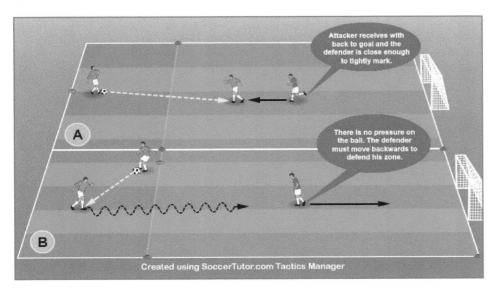

Attacker receives with back to goal and the defender is close enough to tightly mark.

There is no pressure on the ball. The defender must move backwards to defend his zone.

Description

SITUATION A
The first player passes to their teammate who has their back to goal.

The defender is close enough to put pressure on the ball.

The aim for the attacker is to turn and score. The aim for the defender is to prevent a goal.

SITUATION B
The first player passes to their teammate who moves forward with the ball, facing the goal.

The defender is not close enough to apply tight marking and put pressure on the ball. The attacker runs forward and attacks the defender to try and score in the goal. The defender must shift back to defend their zone and close the angle for the attacker to score.

5. Specific Game — 3 Team Possession Game — 20 mins

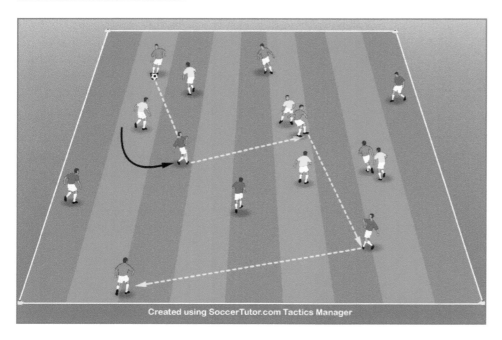

Created using SoccerTutor.com Tactics Manager

Description

We have 3 teams of 5. In an area 30 x 50 yards, 2 teams play a 10v5 possession game against the other team of 5 players.

A point is scored when 10 passes are successfully completed. The objective of the game is to maintain possession, creating space to receive passes.

Change the defending team every 5 minutes.

Coaching Points

1. Good positioning and body shape help to be able to pass the ball first time and speed up play.
2. The defending team need to communicate and apply collective pressure to close off passing angles.

Practice 6   Free Small Sided Game — 20 mins

Individual Tactical Objective: Man marking with and without pressure on the ball.

Technical Objective: Passing with the inside of the foot.

Motor Athletic Objective: Psycho-kinetic specific work: Centre backs and forwards work on explosive power, midfielders work on aerobic power and wide players work on acceleration and deceleration.

Duration of Session: 110 minutes

We recommend starting the session with exercises for general mobility to prevent injuries.

1. Warm Up	**Passing with a Colour Sequence**	**15 mins**

Created using SoccerTutor.com Tactics Manager

Description

Players wear bibs of various colours and pass the ball using a specific sequence decided by the coach (in the diagram for example: red to blue to orange to yellow).

Players play with a maximum of 2 touches. The coach changes the sequence of colours often.

Every 2 minutes stop the play to perform 2 exercises of dynamic stretching.

Variations

1. Use 2 balls at the same time.
2. Play with 1 touch.

Coaching Points

1. Players need to use the correct body shape and positioning to see all possible passing options.
2. Encourage the players to use 1 touch when possible to speed up play.

2. Conditioning — Sprint Training and Quick Dribbling — 20 mins

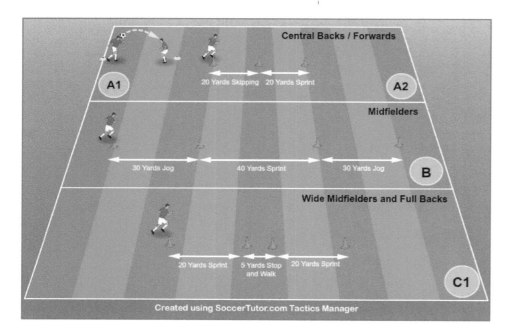

Central Backs / Forwards

20 Yards Skipping   20 Yards Sprint

A1   A2

Midfielders

30 Yards Jog   40 Yards Sprint   30 Yards Jog

B

Wide Midfielders and Full Backs

20 Yards Sprint   5 Yards Stop and Walk   20 Yards Sprint

C1

Created using SoccerTutor.com Tactics Manager

Description

Centre backs and Forwards
A1) Squat holding the position for 10 seconds then heading work in pairs. (2 x 10 repetitions).

2 minutes:
Active recovery while juggling.

A2) 20 yards skipping + 20 yard sprint with the ball. (10 repetitions)

Midfielders
B) 30 yard jog + 40 yard sprint + 30 yard jog. (11 repetitions + 45 seconds recovery).

Full backs and Wide Midfielders
C1) 20 yard sprint, stop and walk 5 yards, 20 yard sprint. (2 x 10 repetitions).

2 minutes:
Recovery.

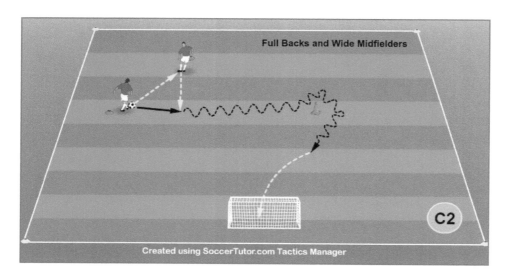

Full Backs and Wide Midfielders

C2

Created using SoccerTutor.com Tactics Manager

C2) The first player passes the ball to their teammate, sprints to receive the ball back, quickly dribbles round the cone and shoots in the small goal.

(5 minutes)

3. Technical   Passing and Receiving Square   15 mins

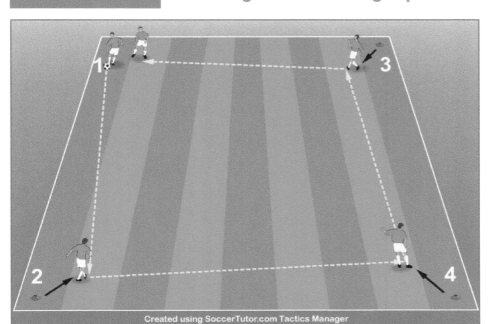

Description

5 players in a square pass the ball in the pattern shown.

Player 1 passes to 2, player 2 to 4, Player 4 to 3 and finally 3 back to the start for the new number 1 to start the sequence again.

Each player moves to the next position after their pass.

Variation

One touch passing

Coaching Points

1. Players should move to meet the ball and approach it half turned.
2. Change the direction of the drill so the players pass and receive with both feet.

4. Game Situation   Defensive Positioning in a 2v2 Situation   20 mins

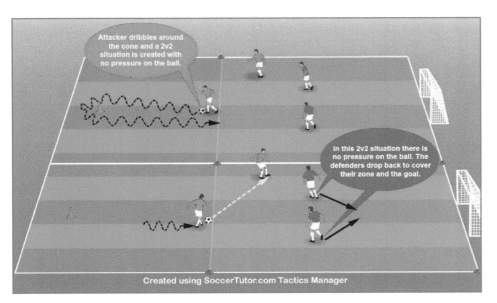

Attacker dribbles around the cone and a 2v2 situation is created with no pressure on the ball.

In this 2v2 situation there is no pressure on the ball. The defenders drop back to cover their zone and the goal.

Description

One of the forwards dribbles the ball backwards round the cone, then runs forwards with the ball to attack the defenders and try to score in the goal.

The defenders must react to this situation in the proper way.

As the forward turns around the cone and faces the goal, a situation with no pressure on the ball arises. The forward can pass the ball to his teammate creating a 2v2 game. The defenders must use the correct reaction, which is to drop back and cover their zone and the goal.

5. Specific Game   2v2 (+2) Possession Game with End Zones   20 mins

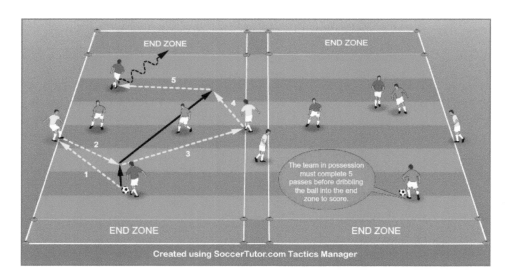

END ZONE

5

4

2

3

1

The team in possession must complete 5 passes before dribbling the ball into the end zone to score.

END ZONE

END ZONE

END ZONE

Created using SoccerTutor.com Tactics Manager

Description

Set up mini fields for games of 2v2 with 2 outside neutral players at the sides.

A goal is scored by dribbling the ball into the end zones, but the team must successfully complete 5 passes before this is allowed.

Coaching Points

1. To maintain possession, the numerical advantage with the neutral players needs to be fully exploited.

2. Encourage one-two combinations and make sure they are quick and sharp.

Practice 6   Free Small Sided Game   20 mins

Individual Tactical Objective: Man marking.

Group Tactical Objective: Providing support while the ball is in the air.

Technical Objective: Passing and shooting.

Motor Athletic Objective: Quickness.

Duration of Session: 110 minutes

We recommend starting the session with exercises for general mobility to prevent injuries.

| 1. Warm Up | 6v6 Penetrating Passes Possession Game | 15 mins |

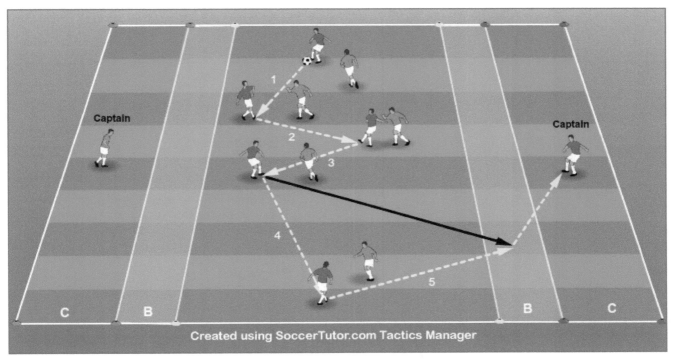

Created using SoccerTutor.com Tactics Manager

Description

Set up a pitch with 5 zones as shown in the diagram.

We play 5v5 is in the middle zone. After 5 passes, the team in possession can pass the ball into the attacking zones (B) for a teammate to run and receive and pass the ball to his captain who is standing 5 yards away in zone C.

If the final pass is successful, the team scoring the goal remains in possession of the ball.

Play 2 halves of 5 minutes with 5 minutes of dynamic stretching in between..

Coaching Points

1. The timing of runs and passes into the B zones are key to this practice.
2. There should be a mixture of passes; to feet, into space and one-two combinations.

2. Conditioning — Circuit training & Technical Work in Pairs Under Condition of Quickness

15 mins

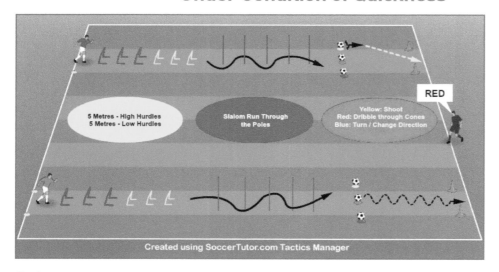

Description

10 minutes
Circuit training: 3 high hurdles + 3 low hurdles + 10 yards of running in between 5 poles.

After the poles, sprint to a colour cone called out by the coach.

Red = Dribble through cones.

Blue = Shoot through cones.

Green = Change of direction.

5 minutes
Juggling and volley passes in pairs under condition of quickness, e.g. Perform 5 squats before receiving the ball.

---

3. Technical — Defensive Support Play from a Long Ball

20 mins

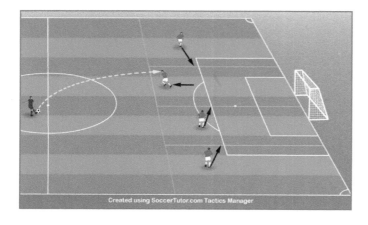

Description

PART 1
Only the defenders are involved in this exercise.

The back 4 train on providing support to the player attacking the ball in the air, as shown in the diagram.

Progression

After 10 minutes introduce 2 forwards, with 1 of them trying to flick the ball on for the other forward who runs into the space in behind.

Description

PART 2
The other players not involved in Part 1 play a 5v5 game with 4 goals. Each team defends 2 goals.

Players use a maximum of 2 touches with the objective of keeping good possession before scoring.

4. Game Situation   1v1 Situations   20 mins

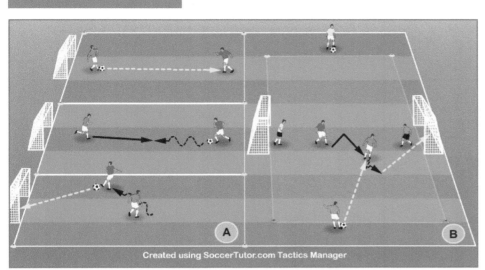

Created using SoccerTutor.com Tactics Manager

Description

EXERCISE A

The defender passes the ball to the attacker and we start the 1v1. The aim for the attacker is to beat the defender and score in the goal.

Use different ways to pass the ball, like along the ground or in the air.`

EXERCISE B

We have a 1v1 situation with 2 goals and 2 goalkeepers. The ball is passed in by the 2 players on the outside. The attacking player must free himself from the defender and call for the ball from one of the outside players.

The colour of the player who passes the ball (orange in diagram) is which goal they must shoot in (orange goalkeeper). If the defender wins the ball he becomes the attacker.

5. Specific Game   1v1 / 2v2 Zonal Defending   20 mins

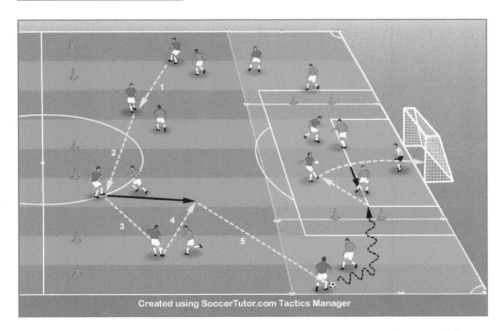

Created using SoccerTutor.com Tactics Manager

Description

After completing 5 passes, the blue team can pass the ball into the side zones (1v1) or the penalty area (2v2).

In the middle zone, the forwards must create space to receive the ball.

In the wide zones, the wingers score a point if they can cross the ball or if they dribbles through the cones and enter the middle zone.

The objective is to score in the goal. If the red team wins the ball, they are able to score by dribbling through one of the 3 goals after completing 5 passes themselves. Change team roles after 10 minutes.

| Practice 6   Free Small Sided Game | 20 mins |

TRAINING UNIT FOR WEEK 11 & 12

Individual Tactical Objective: Creating space.

Group Tactical Objective: Quick counter attacks.

Technical Objective: Penetrating passes.

Motor Athletic Objective: Specific work: Centre backs and forwards work on explosive power, midfielders work on aerobic power and wide players work on acceleration and deceleration.

Duration of Session: 110 minutes

We recommend starting the session with exercises for general mobility to prevent injuries.

| 1. Warm Up | 4v4v4 Dynamic 3 Zone Possession Game | 20 mins |

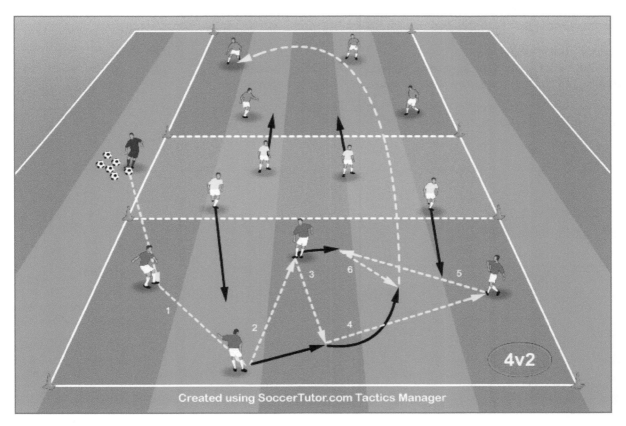

Created using SoccerTutor.com Tactics Manager

Description

Set up a long and narrow area. The objective is to make a lofted pass to the team in the opposite end zone after successfully completing 6 passes.

The coach passes to a team in an end zone and the defending team move 2 players to apply pressure on the team in possession (4v2 as shown).

If a team loses possession or does not complete the lofted pass to the other team, they become the defending team who must apply pressure and try to intercept the ball.

Coaching Points

1. This practice requires all types of passes (short, medium, long, to feet and into space).
2. The defending players need to apply collective pressure to close off the passing angles.

2. Conditioning — Position Specific Training Exercises — 15 mins

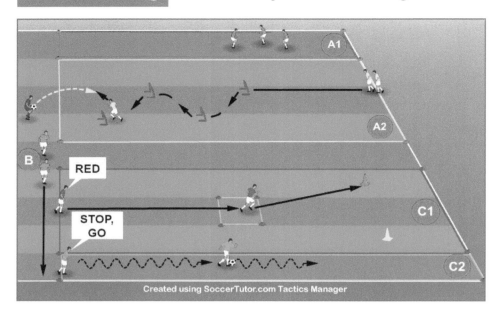

Description

Centre backs and forwards
A1) 4 series of 10 x squats with 30 seconds recovery in between.

A2) Jump over 3 hurdles and at the fourth head the ball launched by the coach (2 x 10 repetitions).

Midfielders
B) 7 minutes running around the field alternating 45 seconds of jogging to 15 seconds sprinting.

(Twice with 2 minutes recovery in between).

Full backs and wide Midfielders
C1) 15 yard sprint, stop in the square and sprint towards the cone called out by a teammate (2 x 10 repetitions with 2 minutes recovery in between).

C2) Running with the ball over 60 yards with teammate calling 'stop' and 'go.' (2 x 5 repetitions with 2 minutes recovery).

3. Technical — 1-2 Combination Play with Close Pressure — 15 mins

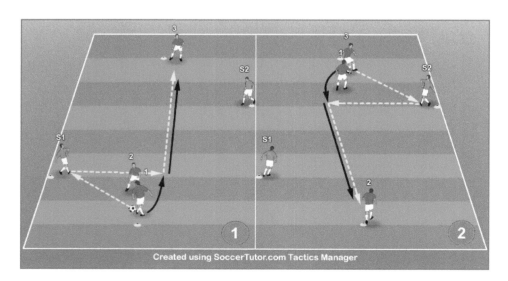

Description

In an area 15 x 10 yards, we have 2 players positioned at the sides.

Player 1 starts by playing a 1-2 combination with the outside player (S1). Player 2 applies passive pressure.

When Player 1 receives the ball back, he passes to Player 2 and moves to apply passive pressure.

Player 3 then starts the same sequence again, as shown in part 2.

Coaching Points

1. The rhythm of the movement together with the pass is key.
2. The second pass of the 1-2 needs to be out in front of the player to run onto and make a 1 touch pass.
3. The side players should move to meet the ball and approach it half turned.

4. Game Situation — Creating a Numerical Advantage (1v1 → 2v1) · 20 mins

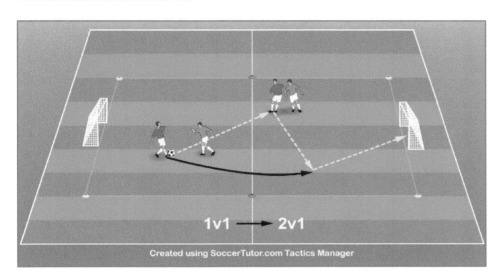

Description

Set out areas of 20 x 10 yards split into 2 zones. In each zone we have a 1v1.

Once the ball is passed to the teammate in the other zone, the player can join in the attack to form a 2v1 situation. The players use this advantage to score.

Variation

2v2 game.

Coaching Points

1. The pass should be made quickly forward, combined with a run into the space.
2. The player waiting in the attacking half should check away from the defender before moving into space to receive.

5. Specific Game — 3v3 (+4) Switching Play with Outside Support Players Possession Game · 20 mins

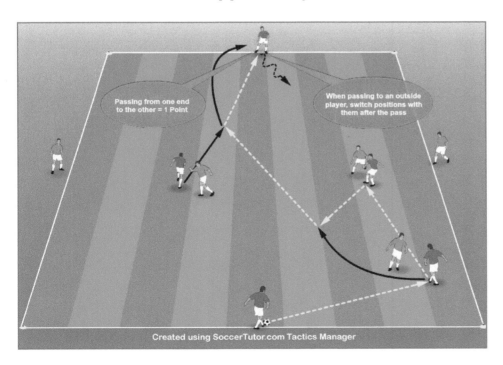

Description

In an area 30 x 30 yards, we play a 3v3 game and each team has 2 additional outside players.

A goal is scored every time the ball is passed from one end to the other end of the area using the outside players.

A player who passes the ball to the outside player then switches with them to take their position.

Practice 6   Free Small Sided Game · 20 mins

Individual Tactical Objective: Creating space.

Technical Objective: Penetrating passes and shooting.

Motor Athletic Objective: Speed of thought: Centre backs and forwards work on explosive power, midfielders work on aerobic power and wide players work on acceleration and deceleration.

Duration of Session: 110 minutes

We recommend starting the session with exercises for general mobility to prevent injuries.

| **1. Warm Up** | **6v3 Speed of Play Dynamic Possession Game** | **15 mins** |

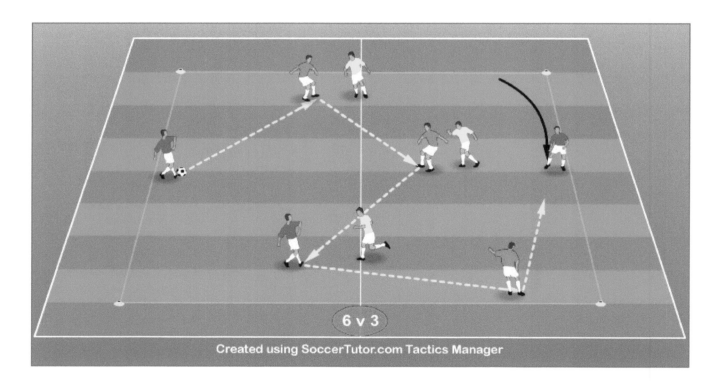

Description

In an area 20 x 20 yards, 2 teams of different colours play against one team creating a 6v3 situation. The objective is to complete 10 continuous passes.

When a player loses possession, his team become the defending team and the other 2 teams aim to complete 10 passes.

Coaching Points

1. The player in possession should always have 2 options so the players need to have intelligent movement to create good angles for the pass.

2. The 3 defenders must press together to close the passing angles making it harder to keep possession.

2. Conditioning   Position Specific Training Exercises (2)   **15 mins**

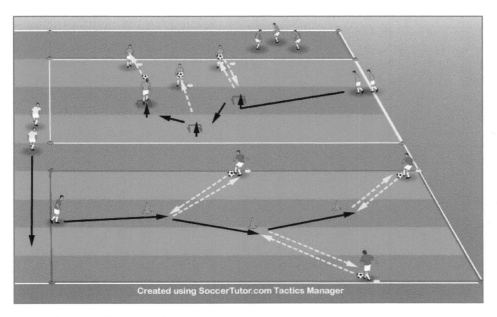

Created using SoccerTutor.com Tactics Manager

Description

Centre backs and forwards
10 squats (5 repetitions) with 30 seconds recovery.

Jump and head the ball 3 times. (2 x 10 repetitions).

Midfielders
7 minutes running around the field, alternating 40 seconds of jogging and 20 seconds sprinting.

2 minutes:
Recovery.

Full backs and wide midfielders
Sprint to the cone, stop and walk to receive and pass the ball to their teammate. Repeat the same to the other cones. (2 x 10 repetitions with 2 minutes recovery).

3. Technical   One-Two Combination and Shot   **20 mins**

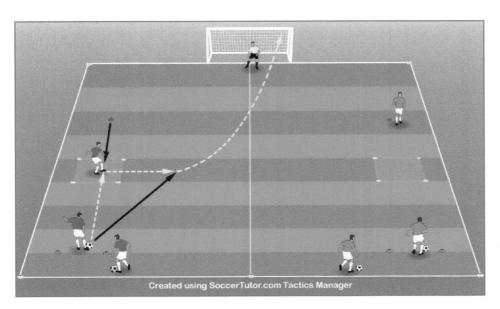

Created using SoccerTutor.com Tactics Manager

Description

2 groups compete in a game of passing and shooting.

Player A passes to B who has moved into the square and he plays a first time pass into the path of A's forward run (1-2 combination).

He receives and shoots at the goal. The team that scores the most goals win.

Variations

1. Limit players to 1 touch for all aspects of the drill.
2. Use a lofted pass into the square to practice receiving ball in the air.

4. Game Situation 3v2 Game with Target Player

20 mins

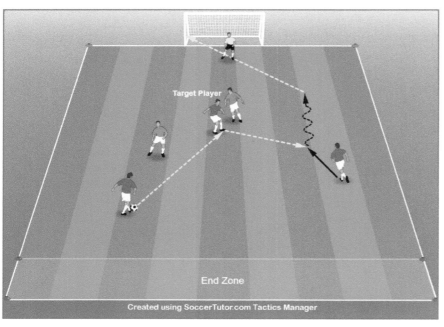

Description

We play games of 3v2 with one of the attacking players playing as a target player who must make a 1 touch pass back to a teammate.

The attacking players try to beat the defenders and score past the goalkeeper.

If the defending team intercept the ball, they can score by dribbling into the end zone.

Coaching Points

1. The target player needs to check away from their marker before moving to receive the ball.

2. The final pass should be made to the player without a marker in space.

5. Specific Game 3v3 (+4) Speed of Play Game with Target Players

15 mins

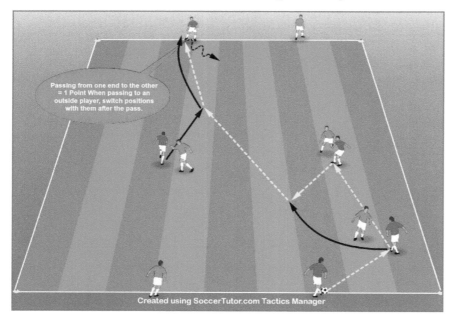

Description

In an area 30 x 30 yards, we play a 3v3 game and each team has a target player at both ends.

A goal is scored every time the ball is passed from one end to the other end of the field using the target players.

Practice 6   Free Small Sided Game

20 mins

Individual Tactical Objective: Creating space.

Group tactical objective: Providing defensive support while the ball is in the air and playing out from the back.

Technical Objective: Passing and shooting.

Motor Athletic Objective: Quickness.

Duration of Session: 110 minutes

We recommend starting the session with exercises for general mobility to prevent injuries.

---

1. Warm Up   5v2 2 Touch Possession Game   15 mins

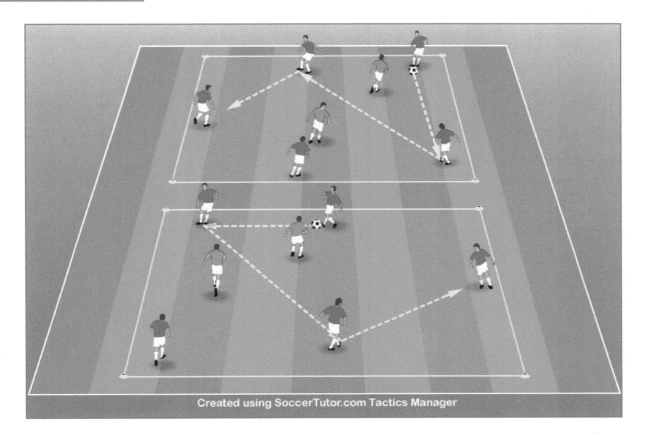

Description

In an area 10 x 10 yards, we play a 5v2 possession game with a maximum of 2 touches.

Play 3 x 3 minute games, with 3 minutes of general mobility and stretching in between the games.

Coaching Points

1. The player in possession should always have 2 passing options so the players need to have intelligent movement to create good angles.

2. The 2 defenders must press together to close the passing angles, making it harder for the attacking team to keep possession.

2. Conditioning   Hurdles, Volley Pass and Sprinting   **15 mins**

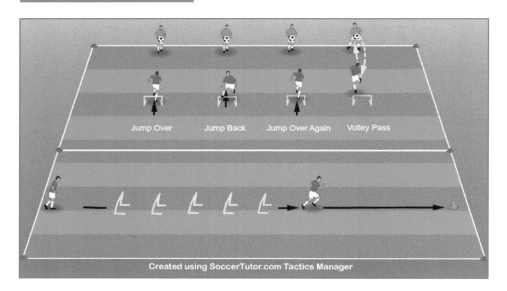

Jump Over   Jump Back   Jump Over Again   Volley Pass

Created using SoccerTutor.com Tactics Manager

Description

A) 5 minutes of technique in pairs under condition of quickness:

Low hurdles (jump over, jump back, jump over again and then execute a volley pass from a teammate's throw).

Each player works for 30 seconds, followed by 5 yards of light jogging.

Players execute the following:
Volley with inside of left/right foot, volley with left/right instep, along the ground, half volley and heading.

B) 3 minutes of jumping over the 5 low hurdles + 5 yard sprint.

---

3. Game Situation   2v1 on the Flanks with Accurate Crossing   **15 mins**

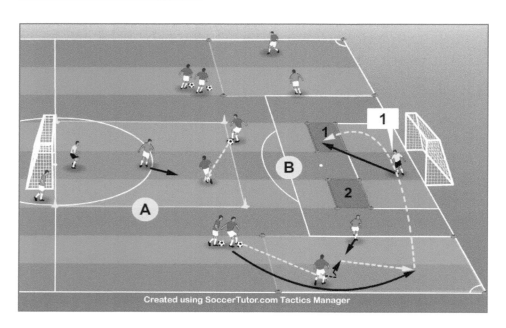

Created using SoccerTutor.com Tactics Manager

Description

A) Central defenders and forwards play a 2v1. The attackers must shoot within 4 seconds.

B) The other players work on situations of 2v1 on the flank with overlapping runs.

The attacking players can score a point if they are able to cross the ball into zone 1 or zone 2 which is called out by the goalkeeper who then moves to catch the ball

Variations for A

1. One forwards starts with his back to goal.

2. One forward enters from the outside making a diagonal run to receive.

4. Tactical Situation — Defensive Support with the Ball in the Air & Build Up Play with 2 Centre Midfielders

20 mins

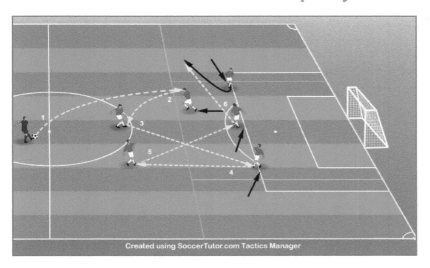

Created using SoccerTutor.com Tactics Manager

Description

We work with the proper movement of the 4 defenders in providing support to the defender attacking the ball in the air. One defender attacks the ball and the other 3 defenders drop off to provide support.

2 central midfielders are introduced to work on building up play from the back.

Variations

1. Build up from the back 4 using the central midfielders.
2. Build up with the central defender breaking through into the midfield line.
3. Moving the ball across the back 4 using the central midfielders

5. Specific Game — 6v6v6 Quick Shooting Game

20 mins

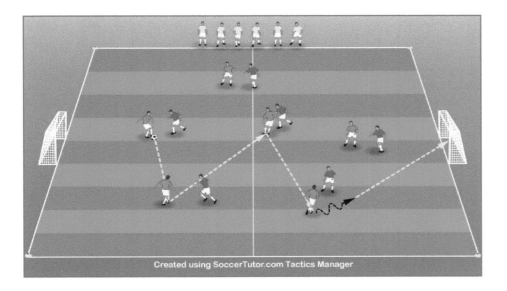

Created using SoccerTutor.com Tactics Manager

Description

We play a 6v6 as shown in the diagram. If a goal is scored within 5 passes the team gets a point.

Every time a team takes a shot on goal that team must leave the field and the team waiting on the sideline enters in their place.

The team that scores the most goals in the 20 minutes win.

Play 2 halves of 8 minutes each. A quick change over is required by the teams.

Variations

1. Goals must be scored from a first time shot.
2. A goal is only allowed after a one-two combination

Practice 6   Free Small Sided Game

20 mins

TRAINING UNIT FOR WEEK 13 & 14

Individual Tactical Objective: Creating space.

Group tactical objective: Ball possession.

Technical Objective: Penetrating passes.

Motor Athletic Objective: Specific work: Centre backs and forwards work on explosive power, midfielders work on aerobic power and wide players work on acceleration and deceleration.

Duration of Session: 110 minutes

We recommend starting the session with exercises for general mobility to prevent injuries.

---

1. Warm Up   5v3 Dynamic Small Sided Game   15 mins

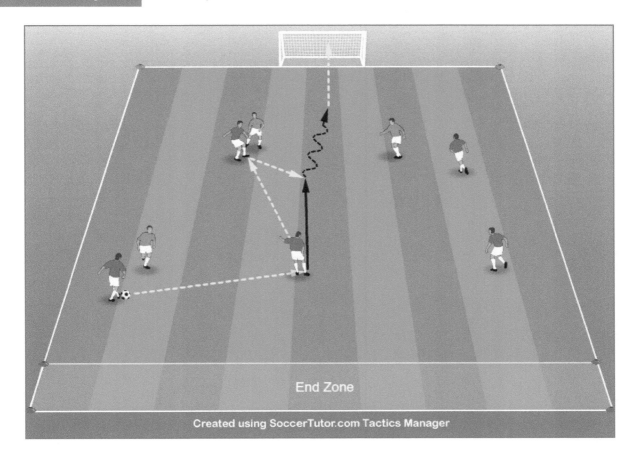

End Zone

Created using SoccerTutor.com Tactics Manager

Description

3 defenders play against 5 attackers. The attacking team scores a point if they make 10 consecutive passes or if they score in the goal.

The defenders take away 2 points to the attacking team if they win the ball and dribble through the end zone.

Variations

1. A maximum of 2 touches for the attacking team.
2. The defender that wins the ball must dribble trough the end zone with no support from their teammates

---

2. Conditioning   Position Specific Training Exercises (3)   **15 mins**

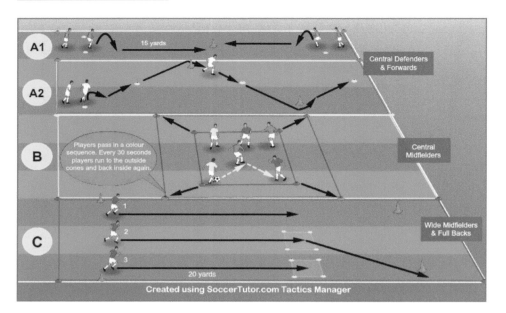

Description

Centre backs and forwards

A1) Counter-movement jump + 15 yard sprint, then 15 seconds recovery. (3 x 10 repetitions)

A2) Counter-movement jump with sprint to first cone, decelerate to next, change direction at traffic cone & sprint, decelerate and change direction to the last cone. (2 x 10 repetitions)

20 seconds recovery between repetitions. 1.5 minutes recovery between each series.

Midfielders (10 repetitions for each)

B) inside the square, players with various colour bibs pass the ball around following a specific colour sequence. Players must be moving at all times. Every 30 seconds players must sprint outside the square to a cone and return inside the circle. We play 2 sets of 6 minutes with 3 minutes recovery.

Full backs and Wide Midfielders

C) 1: 20 yard sprint leaning forward first. 2: 20 yard sprint leaning forward first and then stopping the zone. 3: 20 yard sprint leaning forward, then stopping in zone A and changing direction, sprinting to a cone

---

3. Technical   Diagonal Run with Penetrating Pass   **20 mins**

Description

6 players dribble the ball freely in the centre circle.

Each player has a teammate that dribbles the ball in one of the side zones as shown in the diagram.

One of the side players will decide to leave their zone and their ball to make a run towards a zone just outside the penalty area.

This player must receive a pass from his teammate in the centre circle who should have seen the diagonal run. The pass must be received inside the yellow zone and the player can then shoot at goal.

4. Game Situation   Varying 3v2 Game Scenarios   20 mins

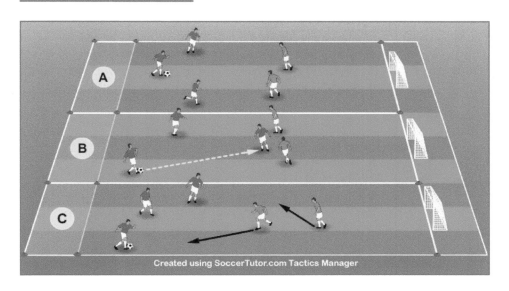

Created using SoccerTutor.com Tactics Manager

Description

A) This is a 3v2 with all the forwards facing he goal. The attacking team has 5 seconds to score a goal. If the defenders win the ball they score by dribbling trough the end zone.

B) This is a 3v2 with one forward receiving the ball with his back to goal. Defenders can score as they can in A.

C) 3v2 with one defender playing as a sweeper behind the other defender. The attacking player in possession of the ball must ensure to pass the ball to the open teammate (utilising the numerical advantage).

5. Specific Game   Passing Conditions in 4v4 SSGs   20mins

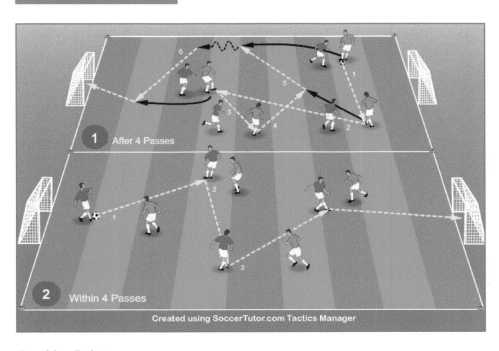

1   After 4 Passes

2   Within 4 Passes

Created using SoccerTutor.com Tactics Manager

Description

4v4 tournament with different conditions.

Game 1: Score a goal after a minimum of 4 passes.

Game 2: Score a goal within 4 passes.

Variations for Game 2

1. Goals must be scored from a first time shot.

2. A goal is only allowed after a 1-2 combination. Practice 6

Coaching Points

1. In Part 1 you can add a condition that all the players need to touch the ball before a goal is scored.

2. In Part 2 the ball needs to be passed quickly forwards to shoot early (emphasis on speed of play).

Practice 6   Free Small Sided Game   20 mins

Individual Tactical Objective: Creating space.

Group tactical objective: Quick play.

Technical Objective: Penetrating passes.

Motor Athletic Objective: Specific work: Centre backs and forwards work on explosive power, midfielders work on aerobic power and wide players work on acceleration and deceleration.

Duration of Session: 115 minutes

We recommend starting the session with exercises for general mobility to prevent injuries.

1. Warm Up	Handball Game	20 mins

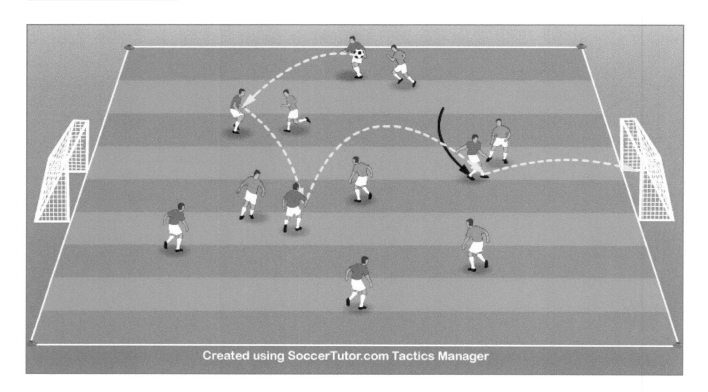

Created using SoccerTutor.com Tactics Manager

Description

In this warm up we play a 6v6 handball game. Players use their hands to throw the ball to each other.

Goals must be scored with a volley. If the player in possession of the ball is touched (tagged) by an opponent the ball is turned over.

Quick play is encouraged.

Variation

Play with hands and feet, kicking the ball out of the hands and catching to pass and receive.

2. Conditioning — Position Specific Training Exercises (4) — 15 mins

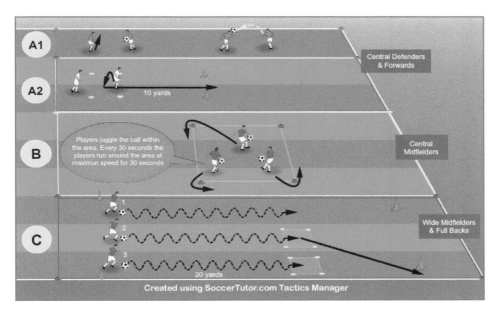

Description

Centre backs and Forwards
A1) In pairs: Squats, holding the position for 10 seconds, then jump and head the ball.

(2 x 20 repetitions each with recovery of 1 minute).

A2) Countermovement jump + 10 yard sprint + stop.

(3 x 10 repetitions with 15 seconds recovery).

1 minute recovery between series.

Midfielders
B) Juggling the ball inside the square. Every 30 seconds the players run around the perimeter of the area at maximum speed for 30 seconds. (2 x 6 minutes with 2 minutes recovery in between).

Full backs and Wide Midfielders (10 repetitions for each exercise)
C) 1: 20 yard sprint leaning forward (with the ball).

2: 20 yard sprint leaning forward with the ball and stop in the square zone.

3. 20 yard sprint leaning forward first with the ball, stop in the square zone and then change direction, sprinting to one of the cones.

---

3. Technical — Aerial Pass, Diagonal Run and Volley — 20 mins

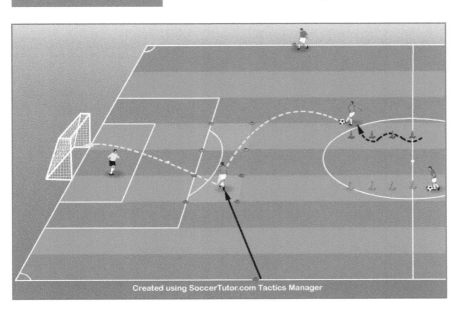

Description

Players dribble the ball around the cones and play a lofted pass into the opposite square where their teammate has made a diagonal run to receive the ball and shoot first time on the volley.

Play from both sides.

Variations

1. Headed finish.
2. Control the ball and shoot.
c. Shoot with a half volley.

4. Game Situation   3v3v3 Speed of Play in the Penalty Area   20 mins

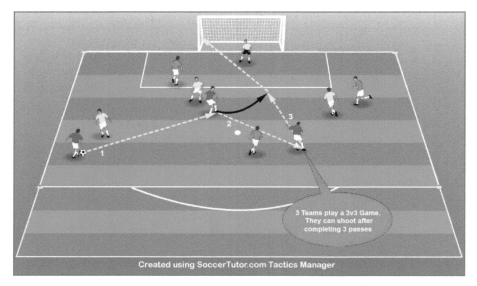

3 Teams play a 3v3 Game.
They can shoot after
completing 3 passes

Created using SoccerTutor.com Tactics Manager

Description

In an area the same size as the penalty area, 3 teams of 3 players play a game.

The condition of the game is to first complete 3 passes and then shoot and score in the goal.

Coaching Points

1. The players need to pass the ball quickly as they have a numerical disadvantage (high speed of play).

2. The timing of the run and the pass is key for the quick attacks which are needed.

3. Shooting at goal should be done with 1 touch as there is limited time and space in this practice.

5. Specific Game   4v4 (+4) SSG with Support Players   20mins

Created using SoccerTutor.com Tactics Manager

Description

Using a long and narrow area, we play 4v4 with 4 neutral support players on the outside who play with the team in possession of the ball.

Variations

1. Limited touches for every player.

2. The support players can pass the ball to each other (as in diagram).

Coaching Point

The players should look to use the outside players as much as possible to exploit the numerical advantage and the extra width to stretch the defending team.

Practice 6 Free Small Sided Game	20 mins

Individual Tactical Objective: Creating space.

Group tactical objective: Providing defensive support while the ball is in the air and build up play from the back.

Technical Objective: Penetrating passes.

Motor Athletic Objective: Speed of thought and quickness.

Duration of Session: 110 minutes

We recommend starting the session with exercises for general mobility to prevent injuries.

| 1. Warm Up | 3v1 Possession Game | 15 mins |

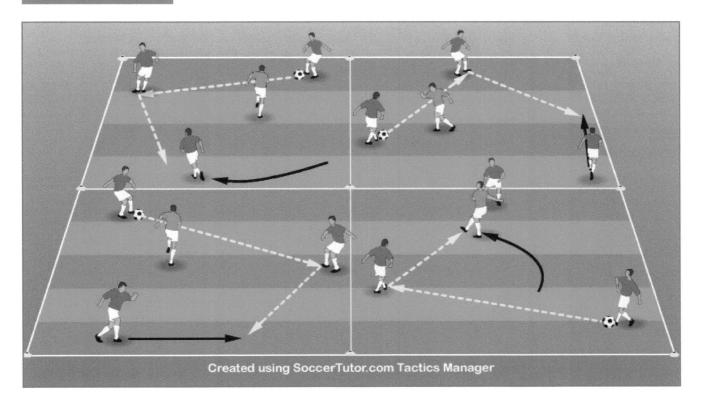

Created using SoccerTutor.com Tactics Manager

Description

We play a 3v1 game with the attacking team aiming to keep possession of the ball.

The defending players try to intercept as many balls as possible in 1 minute.

Work with groups of 5 and change the defender every minute. Allow 1 minute of recovery time for the person who has just stopped the defending role.

Coaching Points

1. The players in possession must always create space by moving along the sides of the square.
2. The defending player must work at a high intensity for the full minute to try and win the ball with this big numerical disadvantage.

2. Conditioning — Hurdle Agility Training & Volley Passes — 15 mins

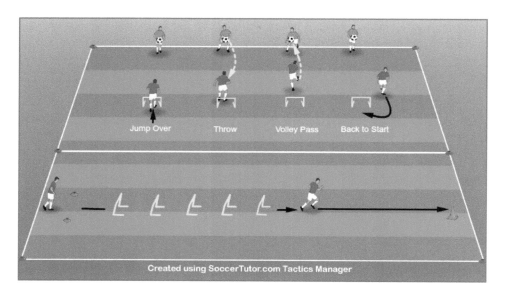

Created using SoccerTutor.com Tactics Manager

Description

A) 3 players work on technique in pairs under condition of quickness:

First, the player jumps over the low hurdle, then volley passes back to their teammate who throws the ball, before returning to the start.

Each player works for 30 seconds

Players execute the following:
Volley with inside of left/right foot, volley with left/right instep, along the ground, half volley and heading.

B) 2 minutes: Jump over 5 low hurdles, followed by 5 yards of light jogging.

3. Technical — Receiving Aerial Passes with 2v1 — 20 mins

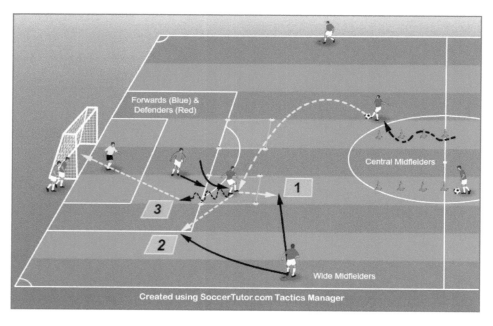

Created using SoccerTutor.com Tactics Manager

Description

Set up the cones as shown in the diagram. The central midfielder dribbles around the cones and plays a lofted diagonal pass into the square determined by the run of the forward who is marked by the defender.

The forward must receive the ball in the square zone which is diagonal to the player making the lofted pass.

The forward has 3 options:

1. Turn and shoot
2. Play a 2v1 with the support of the wide player who has made a diagonal run inside.
3. 2v1 with the wide player making a run down the line.

4. Game Situation — Defensive Support with Ball in the Air Against 2 Forwards

20 mins

The forward players must try to stop the break.

Rules of the game: Always let the forward flick the ball on and the defence must play from the back using short passes to maintain possession of the ball

Description

We work with the proper movement of the 4 defenders in providing support to the defender attacking the ball in the air. 1 defender attacks the ball and the other 3 defenders drop off to provide support.

2 forwards are introduced and 1 tries to flick the ball with his head for the other forward who has run into the space created. If the defenders win the ball they must dribble through the end zone with the support of the central midfielders.

5. Specific Game — 4v4 (+4) with Support Players in the Attacking Zone

20mins

Description

We have 4 teams of 4 and 2 teams play a 4v4 game with 2 goalkeepers. The other 2 teams take up attacking support positions on the outside as shown (2 at the sides and 2 either side of the goal).

The support players must stay in their half and within their area along the touchline or the byline. The aim for the team in possession is to use the support players to score.

Change team roles often

Variations

1. Limited touches for the support players.
2. Play with the hands and volley to score

Practice 6   Free Small Sided Game   **20 mins**

TRAINING UNIT FOR WEEK 15 & 16

Individual Tactical Objective: Creating space.

Technical Objective: Penetrating passes.

Motor Athletic Objective: Psycho-kinetics.

Duration of Session: 105 minutes

We recommend starting the session with exercises for general mobility to prevent injuries.

---

1. Warm Up   **4v4 Target Player Diamond Shape End Zone Game**   **15 mins**

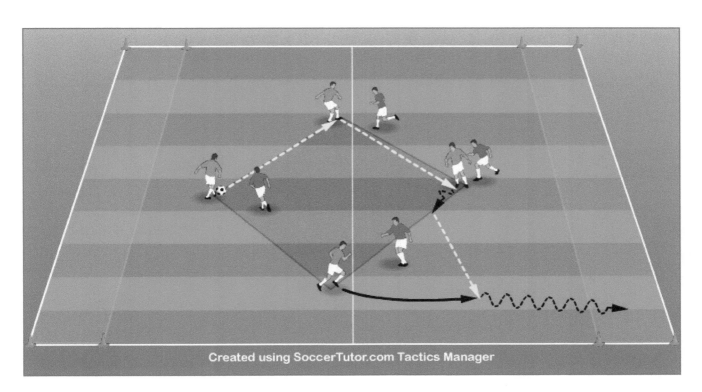

Created using SoccerTutor.com Tactics Manager

Description

We play a 4v4 game with the team in possession maintaining a diamond shape with a target player (front man).

The objective is to score goals by dribbling into the end zones, focusing on combining and playing off of the target player.

Coaching Points

1. Make sure the players use a diamond shape with a target player being utilised at the top.
2. The speed of play should be very high with players making runs off the target player.
3. The players need quick movements and good dribbling technique to dominate the 1v1 situations and enter the end zone.

2. Technical — Short and Long Passing with Colours Between 2 Zones

15 mins

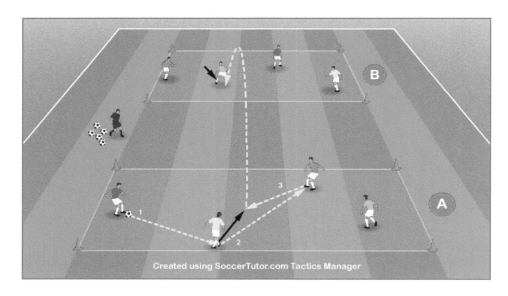

Description

8 players with 4 different colour bibs are in 2 zones.

After 3 passes between players in zone A, the ball is passed in the air to zone B to the player with the same colour of the player in A who did not touch the ball.

Play 5 minutes with one ball and 5 minutes with 2 balls.

Coaching Points

1. The players should try to use all parts of the foot, thigh, chest and head to maximise control of the ball.

2. Limit the players to 1 touch to speed up play and the accuracy of passing required.

3. Technical — Shielding the Ball and Penetrating Passes

20 mins

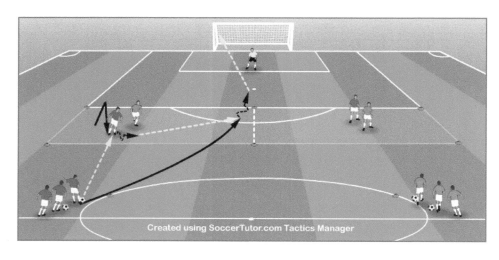

Description

Players are divided in 2 groups and play a 2v1 focusing on penetrating passes.

The forward creates space for himself and makes the movement to receive the ball from his teammate who can join in the attack only after the pass

Coaching Points

1. The correct body shape is required to shield the ball, making sure their body is a barrier between the opponent and the ball.

2. The timing of the run together with the release of the pass is key to this practice.

4. Game Situation — 3v2 Penetrating Passes End Zone Game — 20 mins

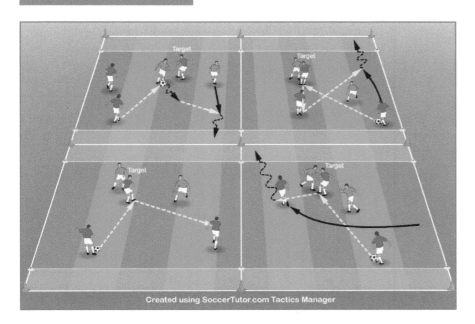

Created using SoccerTutor.com Tactics Manager

Description

Set up pitches where 3v2s are played. One of the forwards acts as a target player. He must receive the ball from the other teammates who then make runs to create space for themselves.

A goal is scored by dribbling through the end zones.

If the defenders intercept the ball and score by dribbling in the other end zone they get 2 points.

Coaching Points

1. The penetrating pass needs to be made to the player in space with no marker.
2. If a defender wins the ball, they should look to use feints/dribbling techniques to dominate a 1v1 situation and dribble the ball into the end zone.

5. Specific Game — Attacking the Space 3 Zone SSG — 20mins

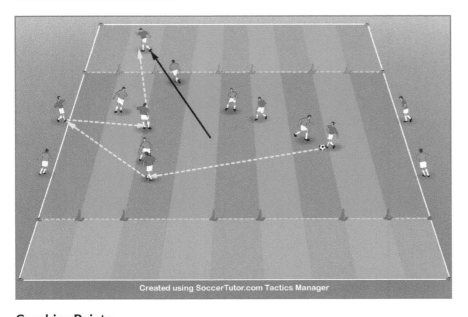

Created using SoccerTutor.com Tactics Manager

Description

Set out a pitch with 3 zones and 6 cone gates as shown in the diagram.

We play 5v5 with 2 support players per team on the sidelines.

A goal is scored when a penetrating pass is made between the cones into the end zone and a teammate makes a run to receive the pass in the end zone.

Coaching Points

1. Good and quick decision making is required for this attacking the space/final ball practice.
2. The rhythm and timing of the runs with the pass is key to good attacking combinations.

Practice 6 — Free Small Sided Game — 20 mins

Individual Tactical Objective: Creating space.

Technical Objective: Passing and ball control.

Motor Athletic Objective: Coordination skills of adaptation, transformation, differentiation and orientation.

Duration of Session: 110 minutes

We recommend starting the session with exercises for general mobility to prevent injuries.

1. Warm Up — Juggling in Pairs — 15 mins

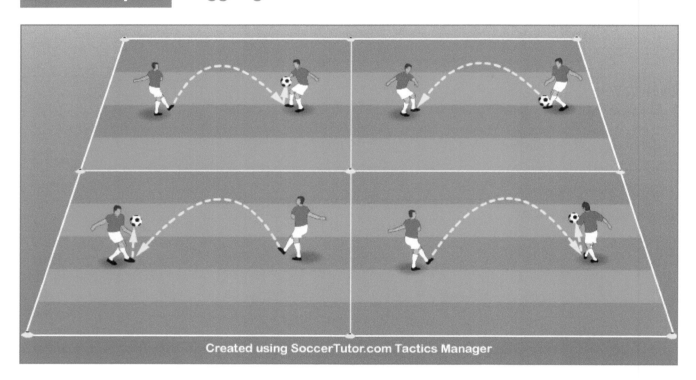

Created using SoccerTutor.com Tactics Manager

Description
The players perform various type of juggling in pairs.

Variations
1. Free touches.
2. Maximum of 2 touches.
3. Only with the head, chest and feet.
4. Juggle with 2 balls.
5. Mandatory use of the thigh to receive the ball.
6. Use balls of various sizes/weights.

Coaching Points
1. Use all parts of the feet, thighs, chest and head to maximise control of the ball.
2. Passes should have good height to maintain a 'rally' between the 2 players.

2. Conditioning — Juggling Coordination Team Game — 15 mins

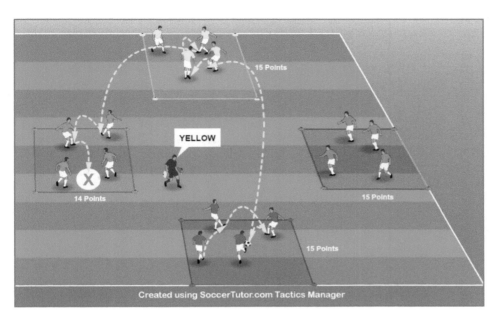

In this game we have 4 teams in 4 separate coloured zones. Each team starts with 15 points and the team that has the most points at the end wins.

There is 1 ball and the team in possession pass the ball to each other in the air. If the ball hits the ground, that team loses 1 point.

The players wait for the coach's call or visual signal to tell them which colour team to pass the ball to next.

Variations

1. Limit the players to 2 touches each.
2. Limit the players to just 1 touch each.

3. Technical — Quick Passing and 1-2 Combinations — 20 mins

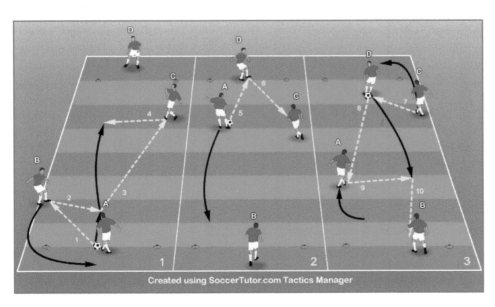

Description

Player A plays a 1-2 with B, then plays another 1-2 with Player C and finally passes to Player D.

D repeats the same combination with C and then A (who has moved back) as shown in the diagram.

Variation

Passes in the air with the players further apart

Coaching Points

1. The rhythm of the movement together with the pass is key.
2. The side players need to display good timing of movement to meet the ball and approach it half turned.

4. Game Situation   2v2 (+2) Game / Double 2v2 Game   20 mins

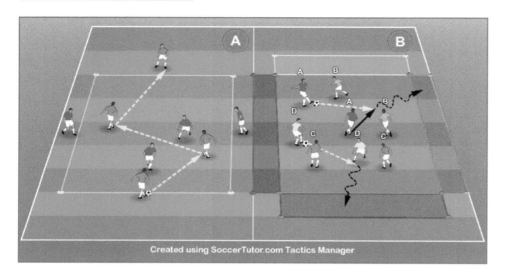

Created using SoccerTutor.com Tactics Manager

Description

A) In an area 10 x 10 yards we play a 2v2 game with 2 support players on the outside for the team in possession of the ball.

A point is scored every time the ball is passed from one support player to the other using the inside players.

B) A double 2v2 is played with team A playing against team B from right to left and team C playing against team D from top to bottom. Use 2 balls in this game.

5. Specific Game   Passing Conditions Small Sided Game   20mins

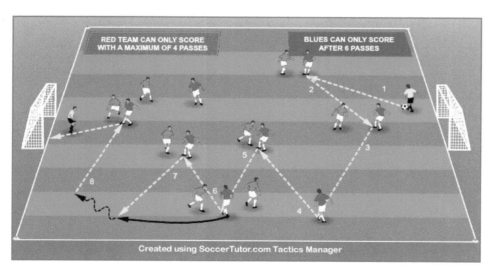

RED TEAM CAN ONLY SCORE WITH A MAXIMUM OF 4 PASSES

BLUES CAN ONLY SCORE AFTER 6 PASSES

Created using SoccerTutor.com Tactics Manager

Description

One team must play with the aim of possession and can only shoot after completing 6 passes.

The other team instead must score using a maximum of 4 passes.

Change the roles of the teams every 5 minutes.

Coaching Points

1. For the blue team, you can add a condition that all players must touch the ball before a goal is scored.

2. The red team need to pass the ball forwards quickly to shoot early (emphasis on speed of play).

Practice 6   Free Small Sided Game   20 mins

Individual Tactical Objective: Creating space.

Group tactical objective: Defensive movements of the back 4.

Technical Objective: Passing.

Motor Athletic Objective: Quickness.

Duration of Session: 110 minutes

We recommend starting the session with exercises for general mobility to prevent injuries.

---

1. Warm Up   3 Team Possession Game   15 mins

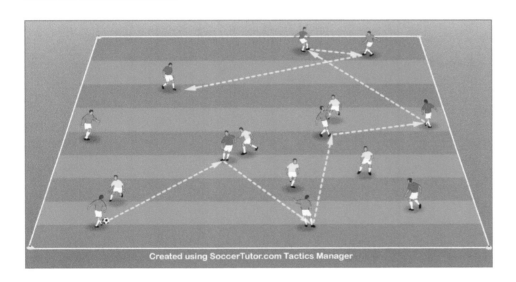

Created using SoccerTutor.com Tactics Manager

Description

We have 3 teams of 5 players each. 2 teams play against the other team with the aim of maintaining possession.

The only objective for the defending team is to win the ball. Every team will defend for 5 minutes. The winning team is the team that allows the least amount of passes while defending.

---

2. Conditioning   Agility Exercise with Volley Passing   15 mins

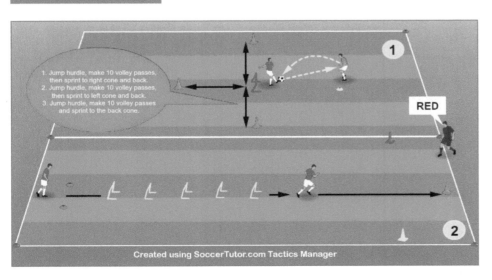

1. Jump hurdle, make 10 volley passes, then sprint to right cone and back.
2. Jump hurdle, make 10 volley passes, then sprint to left cone and back.
3. Jump hurdle, make 10 volley passes and sprint to the back cone.

RED

Created using SoccerTutor.com Tactics Manager

Description

1) The player jumps over the first hurdle and makes 10 volley passes, sprints to the right cone and back.

He then jumps the hurdle and makes 10 volley passes, sprints to the left cone and back. Finally, the player makes 10 volley passes and sprints back to the starting cone. (4 repetitions each)

2) Jump over 5 low hurdles and sprint to the cone.

3. Game Situation   4v2 Support Play End to End Game   20 mins

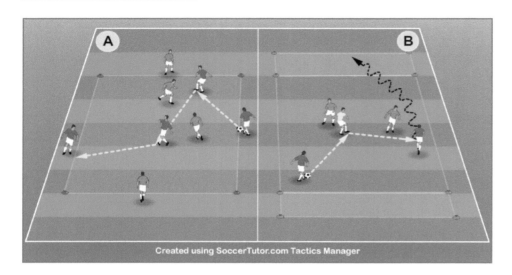

Description

A) In an area 10 x 10 yards, we have 2v2 inside the square and each team has 2 support players each on the outside.

This creates a 4v2 situation. A point is scored when the ball is passed from 1 support player to the other passing through the 2 midfielders. (Play for 10 minutes)

B) In the same size area we have a 2v2 with 1 neutral player who plays with the team in possession.

The teams score by dribbling through the end zone, but both players must have touched the ball.

4. Tactical Situation   Cohesive movement of the Defensive Unit with No Immediate Pressure on the Ball   20mins

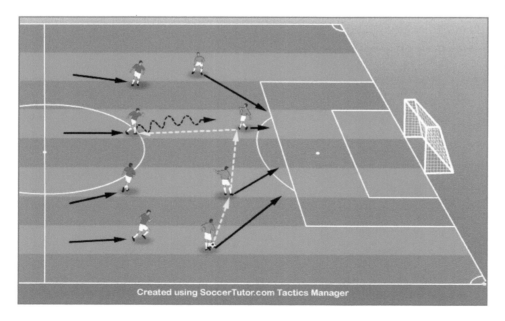

Description

Set up the back 4 line with 4 midfielders starting on the halfway line. The back 4 build up the play using the full width and then voluntarily give the ball to the midfielders.

The player receiving the ball will attack the space in front of him and the back 4 will run backwards delaying the action of the midfielder, until they reach the edge of the penalty area.

At this point they close the space using the proper zonal defensive movements.

Coaching Point

Start by blowing a whistle (or visual signal) to instruct the players when to stop running backwards before progressing to them communicating and organising the defensive line themselves.

5. Specific Game | Fast Break Attacks Dynamic Transition Game | 20 mins

Part A

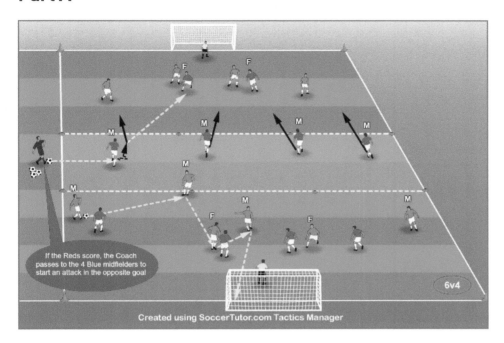

If the Reds score, the Coach passes to the 4 Blue midfielders to start an attack in the opposite goal

6v4

Created using SoccerTutor.com Tactics Manager

Description

We play a 3 zone transition game which creates a 6v4 situation at both ends of the pitch.

The coach starts the drill by passing the ball to one of the team's midfield players in the central zone. They create a 6v4 situation with their 2 forwards and attack the opposition's 4 defenders trying to score a goal.

If the team scores a goal, the coach plays a new ball in for 1 of the opposition's 4 midfielders to start a new attack at the opposite end.

Part B

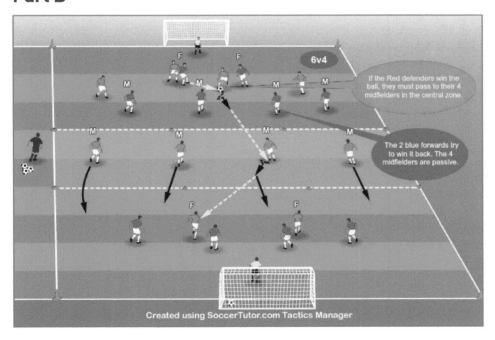

6v4

If the Red defenders win the ball, they must pass to their 4 midfielders in the central zone.

The 2 blue forwards try to win it back. The 4 midfielders are passive.

Created using SoccerTutor.com Tactics Manager

If the defenders win the ball, they must pass the ball into the central zone for their 4 midfielders. The 2 blue forwards try to win the ball back from the defenders, but the midfielders must remain passive.

If the defenders succeed in passing the ball to their midfielders another 6v4 attack starts down the other end.

If the 2 forwards win the ball from the defenders, the 4 midfielders become active again and continue their 6v4 attack at that end.

An unsuccessful shot at goal at anytime results in the turn over of possession to the other team.

| Practice 6 Free Small Sided Game | 20 mins |

TRAINING UNIT FOR WEEK 17 & 18

Individual Tactical Objective: Creating space and crossing.

Technical Objective: Long Passes.

Motor Athletic Objective: Anaerobic endurance.

Duration of Session: 110 minutes

We recommend starting the session with exercises for general mobility to prevent injuries.

| 1. Warm Up | 4v4 with Long Accurate Passing | 15 mins |

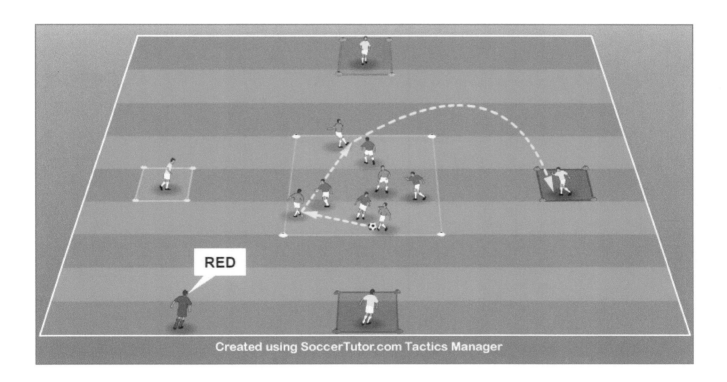

RED

Created using SoccerTutor.com Tactics Manager

Description

We play a 4v4 possession game in the centre square (20 x 20 yards).

The players wait for the coach to call out a colour and the player in possession of the ball must send a long pass to one of the players in that coloured zone.

A point is scored if the player in the coloured zone successfully receives the pass within the zone.

Coaching Points

1. Correct body shape (open up on the half turn) and positioning is important to view where the next pass goes in the centre square.
2. The lofted pass should be highly accurate and have good height for ease of receiving the ball.
3. The player receiving the lofted pass should utilise all parts of the body to maximise control.

2. Conditioning   Running With and Without the Ball in Pairs   15 mins

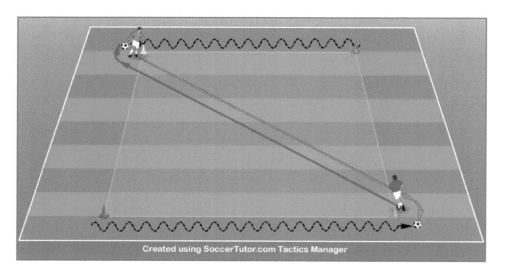

Description

As shown in the diagram, both players run with the ball to the cones in front of them.

They then leave the ball and sprint towards the yellow and orange cones respectively.

Here they start dribbling with the ball again to the next cone (blue and red) and sprint diagonally again from that point.

(Repeat 4 times with recovery times of 1.5 minutes)

3. Technical   Accurate Aerial Passing in Pairs   20 mins

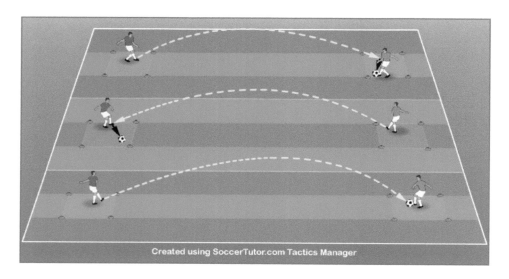

Description

The blue player makes a long pass in the air to the red player and vice-versa.

If a player does not control the ball within the square, the other player gets a point.

If a pass misses the zone, then the player who played the pass loses a point.

Coaching Points

1. The players should try to use all parts of the foot, thigh, chest and head to maximise control of the ball.
2. The aerial passes need to be accurate and played at the right height to receive the ball within the square.
3. Players need to keep their eyes fixed on the flight of the ball, watching it all the way to their foot.

4. Game Situation   Receiving a Long pass & Shielding the Ball   20 mins

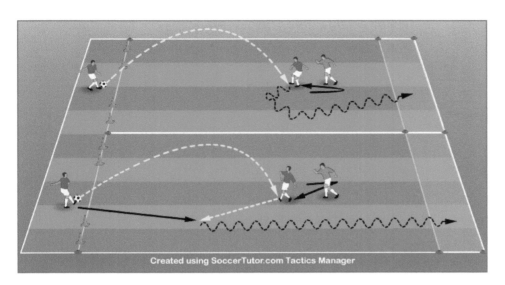

Created using SoccerTutor.com Tactics Manager

Description

The first player makes a long pass to his teammate who can receive the ball and shield it for 5 seconds or play a first time pass back to his teammate.

The player receiving the ball must check away from their marker, making a short movement followed by a longer movement to receive (as shown).

The attacking players must score by dribbling into the end zone.

If the defender intercepts the ball, they can score in one of the 2 mini goals at the other end.

5. Specific Game   Long Passing, Crossing and Finishing in a 7 Zone Small Sided Game   20mins

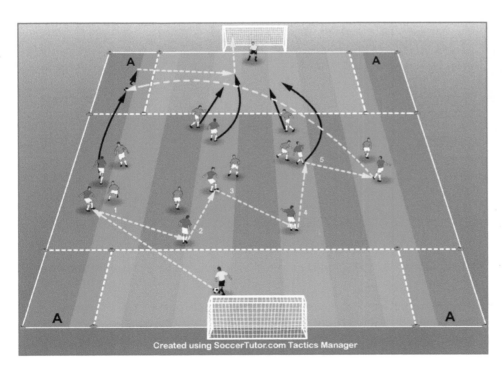

Created using SoccerTutor.com Tactics Manager

Description

Using the area from penalty box to penalty box, we set up 7 zones as shown in the diagram.

After completing 5 passes the team in possession of the ball can make a long pass into one of the 2 zone A's where one player can run into without any defensive pressure.

The player receiving the ball in zone A must cross the ball into zone B where only 2 attackers and 1 defender are allowed in.

Practice 6   Free Small Sided Game   20 mins

SESSION
26

Individual Tactical Objective: Creating space.

Technical Objective: Long passes.

Motor Athletic Objective: Speed endurance.

Duration of Session: 120 minutes

We recommend starting the session with exercises for general mobility to prevent injuries.

| **1. Warm Up** | **4v4 (+4) Long Passing Game with Support Players and Goalkeepers** | **15 mins** |

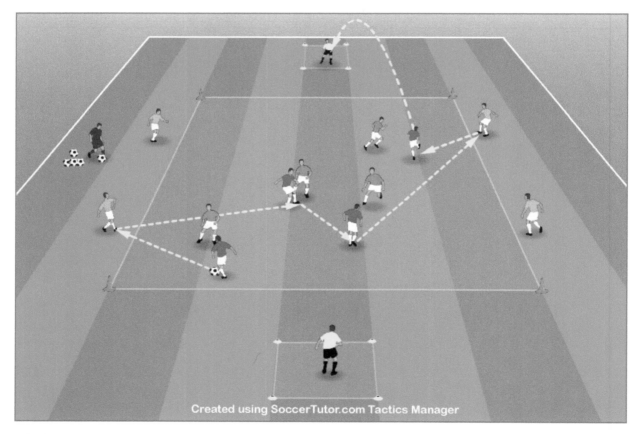

Description

We have a 4v4 game in the middle square with 4 neutral support players on the outside, who play with the team in possession.

The objective is to create space to receive the ball and make a long pass to the goalkeepers who are standing 15 yards away from the square. If the goalkeeper successfully controls the ball, that team wins a point.

Coaching Points

1. The team in possession should make sure to take advantage of the full width by switching play from one neutral side player to the other (stretch the opposition & utilise the numerical advantage).

2. The aerial passes need to be accurate and played at the right height to receive the ball within the square.

2. Conditioning — Sprinting and Changing Direction

15 mins

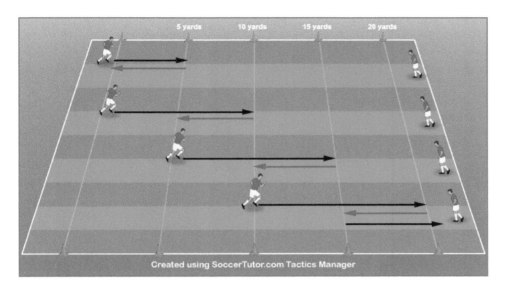

Description

The players perform the sprints between the distances as shown in the diagram.

Repeat these sprints 10 times. Have 30 seconds of recovery time between each repetition.

Repeat the whole series of 10 repetitions twice and have a recovery time of 1 minute.

3. Technical — Receiving Long Passes on the Move

20 mins

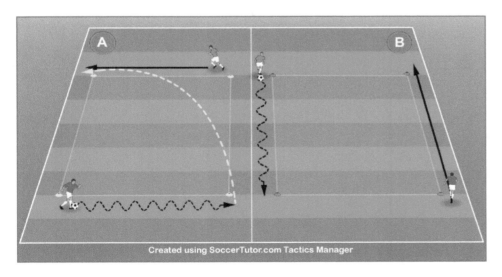

Description

Set up 20 x 20 yard areas. 2 players are in each square working on long passes and receiving the ball.

The blue player dribbles the ball to the next cone and plays a long diagonal pass to the red player who receives and dribbles to the next cone. He performs the same pass.

Coaching Points

1. The pass needs to be well timed and weighted for their teammate to be able to receive the ball on the run without having to stop, making a quick transition into dribbling the ball forwards.

2. Start off at a slow tempo for this practice and then speed up as they improve their timing.

4. Game Situation — Receiving a Long Straight Pass with a 2v1 Play in the Penalty Area

25 mins

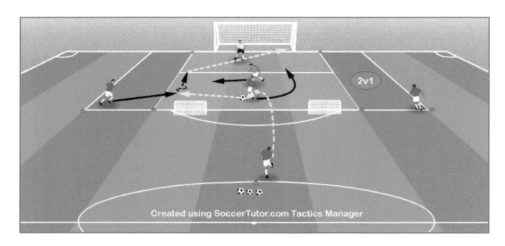

Created using SoccerTutor.com Tactics Manager

Description

One player makes a long pass into the box. The player receiving the ball plays a first time pass to one of the 2 supporting wide players and they play a 2v1 trying to score in the goal.

If the defender intercepts the ball he can score in one of the 2 mini goals

Coaching Points

1. The player receiving the first pass must make his body a barrier between the ball and the defender, making sure to shield the ball so he can lay off a pass to one of the support players.

2. The defender must commit to closing down the supporting player, preventing a free shot on goal.

5. Specific Game — Switching Play with Long Passes in a 7v7 Small Side Game

20mins

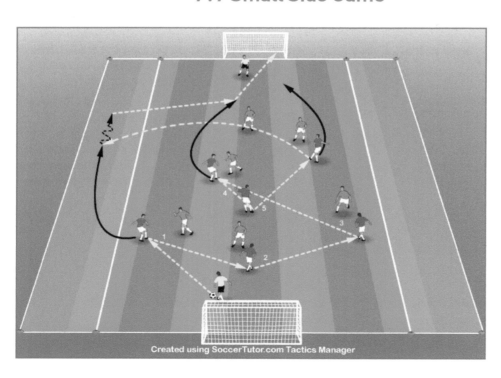

Created using SoccerTutor.com Tactics Manager

Description

We play a 7v7 game. The team in possession can make a long pass into the side zones after completing 5 passes.

A player runs from behind without being challenged by any defenders to receive the pass.

If the pass is successful and the wide player receives correctly he can cross the ball.

Teams get 2 points for a goal from a cross.

Practice 6   Free Small Sided Game

20 mins

Individual Tactical Objective: Creating space and diagonal runs.

Technical Objective: Attacking and defending with build up play from the back.

Motor Athletic Objective: Quickness.

Duration of Session: 110 minutes

We recommend starting the session with exercises for general mobility to prevent injuries.

| 1. Warm Up | 2v2 + Neutral Player End Zone Game | 15 mins |

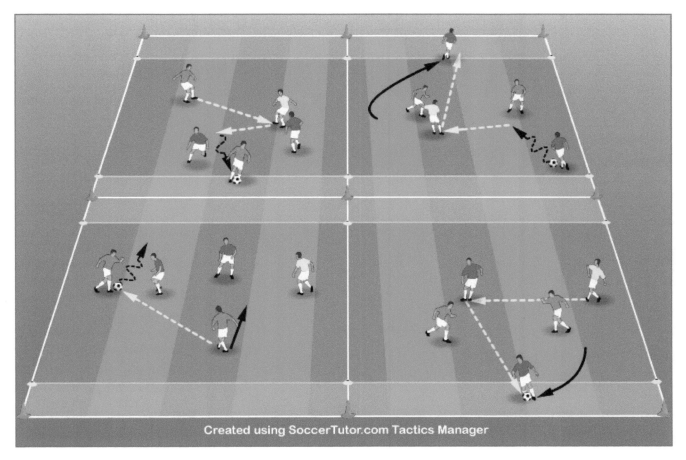

Created using SoccerTutor.com Tactics Manager

Description

Set up many pitches with teams playing 2v2 with an additional neutral player who plays with the team in possession.

The players must make 2 or 3 passes before they can score, which they do by dribbling through the end zones.

Variations

1. Unlimited touches.
2. Limit the players to 2 touches.

2. Conditioning   Speed and Agility Circuit Training

15 mins

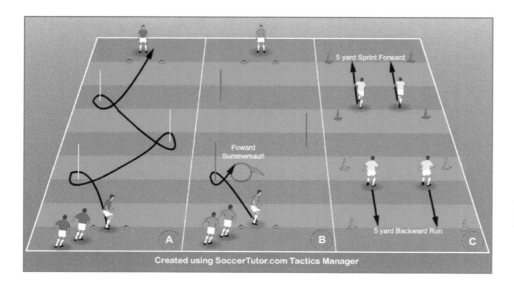

Description

EXERCISE A
15 yard diagonal movements and quick turns around the poles. (10 repetitions)

EXERCISE B
15 yard diagonal movements and quick turn around the pole with summersault. (5 repetitions)

EXERCISE C
5 yard backward run and then 5 yard sprint forwards.

---

3. Technical   Dynamic Quick Reactions 2v2 Game

20 mins

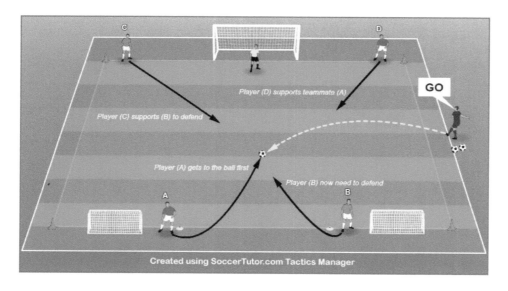

Description

Players A and B have their backs to goal. On the coach's call, they must turn and the first player to the ball can pass to either player C or D who becomes their teammate.

The other player becomes a defender with the player who arrived second to the ball.

We then have a 2v2 situation with the aim to score past the goalkeeper. If the defending team win the ball, they can score in the 2 mini goals.

Variations

1. Use a visual signal.
2. Make the first pass with a volley.
3. Make the first pass with a header.

4. Game Situation — Shooting With and Without Pressure — 20 mins

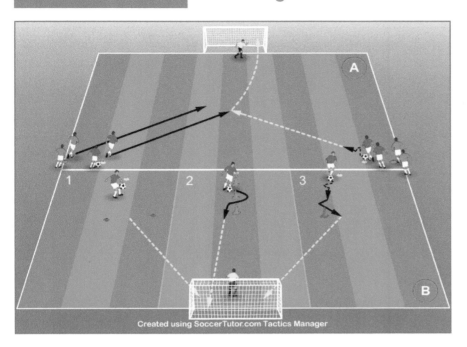

Description

EXERCISE A

The wide player makes a diagonal run to receive the ball in the centre and shoot on goal with pressure from the defender who starts from a slightly outside position.

EXERCISE B

Various shooting drills:

1. Juggle and then shoot.
2. Dribble through the cones and shoot.
3. Dribble (feint) and shoot.

Variations for Exercise A

1. Make the defenders fully active.
2. Aerial pass.

Variations for Exercise B

1. Only use the left or right foot.
2. Only use instep, inside or outside of foot

5. Specific Game — 4v6 to 6v4 Zonal Defending Practice — 20mins

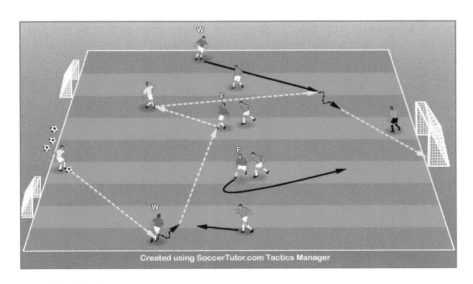

Description

4 defenders play against 4 midfielders and 2 forwards.

The defenders work on zonal defending and if they win the ball they can score in the 2 mini goals at the other end.

They can play the ball into the 2 yellow players who become their centre midfielders.

The opposition forwards and wingers then defend, trying to stop the break ending in a goal.

Coaching Points

1. The players need to maintain their positions to keep the team's shape.
2. Quick reactions are needed in the transitions from attack to defence and defence to attack.

Practice 6   Free Small Sided Game — 20 mins

TRAINING UNIT FOR WEEK 19 & 20

Individual Tactical Objective: Creating space and support play.

Group tactical objective: Movements of centre backs and centre midfielders.

Technical Objective: Passing and receiving.

Motor Athletic Objective: Anaerobic endurance.

Duration of Session: 125 minutes

We recommend starting the session with exercises for general mobility to prevent injuries.

---

1. Warm Up	5v5 Support Play Possession Game	20 mins

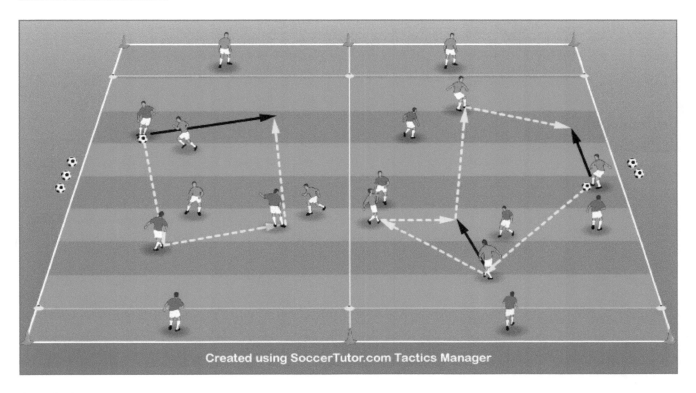

Created using SoccerTutor.com Tactics Manager

Description

In an area 20 x 20 yards, we have a 4v4 in the main area and each team has 1 player in a supporting role at one end.

A point is scored every time 10 passes are completed and every time the ball is passed to the supporting player and successfully received back from them.

Coaching Points

1. The supporting player needs to be constantly moving to create angles to receive the ball.
2. Correct body shape (open up on the half-turn) and positioning is important to view the options for where the next pass is going.

2. Conditioning — 3 Minute Runs with 3 Minutes Recovery — 20 mins

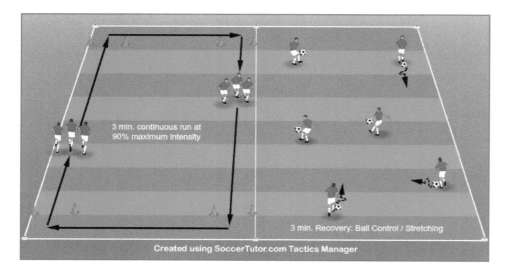

Description

3 minutes of continuous running at 90% intensity.

Repeat 3 times with 3 minutes recovery in between runs.

---

3. Technical — Creating Angles of Support with Proper Movements of Centre Backs and Centre Midfielders — 20 mins

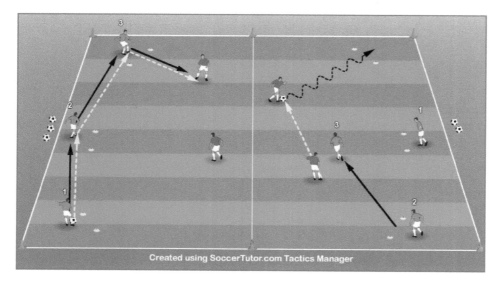

Description

In each area we have 3 mini goals with 3 players standing behind the goals (cones) passing to each other. The outside player (red) plays the ball to the closest inside player (blue) and applies pressure.

The player receiving the ball must pass to his teammate who is in a support position and he must score in the mini goal that has been left unattended as the red players have all shifted across to the next position.

Coaching Points

1. The blue player's pass needs to be quick and out in front of their teammate so they can quickly dribble through the cones before being tackled.

2. The red player must quickly sprint to close down the ball carriers.

4. Game Situation — 2v1 (+2) One-Two Combinations in an End to End Small Sided Game

20 mins

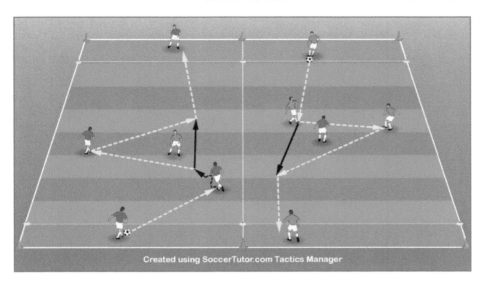

Created using SoccerTutor.com Tactics Manager

Description

We set up various itches where we play 2v1 games with 2 support players in the end zones for the players in possession.

A point is scored every time the ball is passed from one support player to the other but only after a 1-2 combination has been completed (as shown).

Coaching Points

1. The correct angle and distance of the support player's positioning/movement is important in this practice.

2. Start with 2 touches and quickly progress to 1 to speed up play.

5. Specific Game — 5v5 Support Player End Zone Game

20mins

Created using SoccerTutor.com Tactics Manager

Description

In an area 30 x 30 yards, we play a 5v5 game. A goal is scored by dribbling through the end zone.

The players are not allowed to pass forwards.

They must use the pass to the support player to gain the open space and dribble into the end zone.

Coaching Points

1. The angle and distance of the supporting player's positioning/run is the focus in this game.

2. Encourage the players to use feints/dribbling techniques in the 1v1 situations to enter the end zone.

Practice 6   Free Small Sided Game   **20 mins**

SESSION 29

Individual Tactical Objective: Creating space and support play.

Technical Objective: Ball control and shooting.

Motor Athletic Objective: Speed endurance.

Duration of Session: 115 minutes

We recommend starting the session with exercises for general mobility to prevent injuries.

| 1. Warm Up | Pass and Move Sequence with 3 Players | 20 mins |

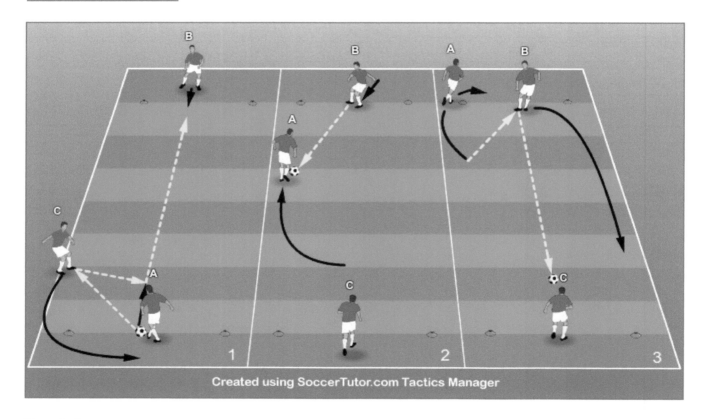

Created using SoccerTutor.com Tactics Manager

Description

As shown in the diagram, player A passes to C who returns the ball to A. A then passes to player B and moves to provide angled support. Player C takes up A's position.

Player B passes to A who returns the ball to B. B then passes to player C and moves to provide angled support. Player A takes up B's position. Player C then repeats the sequence with the first pass to B.

Variations

1. Unlimited touches.
2. Maximum of 2 touches.
3. One touch play.
4. Play with aerial passing.

2. Conditioning — Sprinting with Visual Awareness and Wind Sprints

15 mins

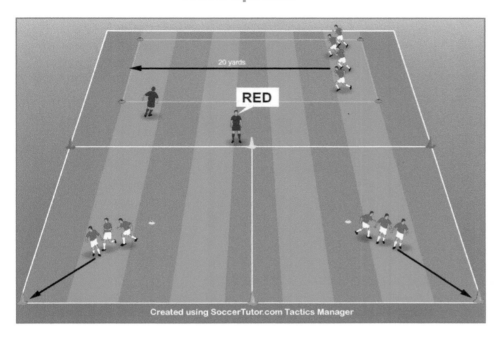

Description

EXERCISE 1
Wind sprints over 20 yards. (10 repetitions with 15 seconds recovery).

Repeat twice with 1 minute recovery in between.

EXERCISE 2
The players sprint towards the colour cone called out by the coach and lightly jog back.

(5 x 10 repetitions)

3. Technical — Shooting After Dribbling Inside

20 mins

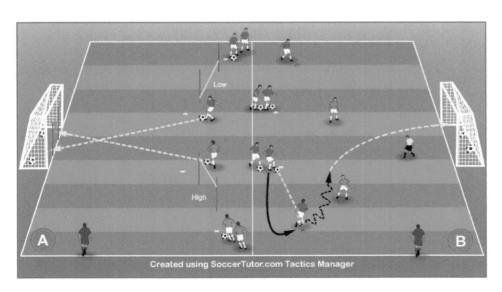

Description

EXERCISE A
On both sides a string is placed between 2 poles, one 30 cm high and the other 120 cm high.

The players must dribble the ball and skip over the string or duck under it. They then shoot the ball in the goal.

EXERCISE B
The players dribble the ball forwards and beat the passive defender, before shooting past the goalkeeper.

Variations for Exercise B

1. Juggling the ball.
2. Beat the defender with a nutmeg.
3. Beat the player with a pre-determined feint/move to beat e.g. step over, double step over.

4. Game Situation — 5v3 Dynamic Possession Game with Target Goalkeeper

20 mins

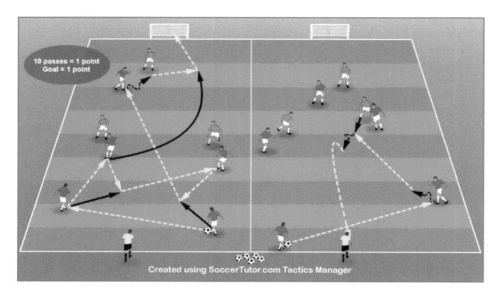

Description

We play a 5v3 game with a goalkeeper at one end playing with the team of 3 players.

The team of 5 players score a point when they complete 10 passes or every time they score in the small goal.

The team with 3 players scores a goal every time the ball is passed to the goalkeeper.

Change roles often.

Coaching Points

1. The defenders need to keep a good shape and defend their zone collectively.
2. They must actively try to win the ball and make a fast transition to attack.

5. Specific Game — 4v4 Games with Passing Conditions (2)

20mins

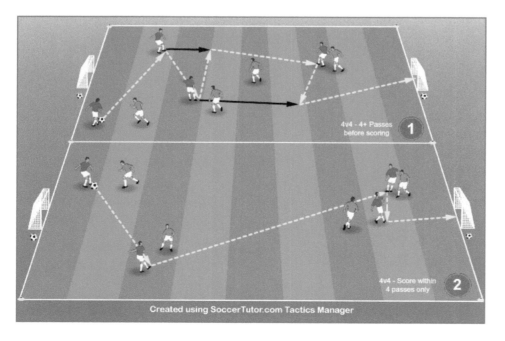

Description

Here we play a 4v4 tournament with different passing conditions.

GAME 1
A goal only be scored after the team has completed 4 passes.

GAME 2
A goal must be scored within 4 passes

Practice 6   Free Small Sided Game

20 mins

Individual Tactical Objective: Creating space and counter-movements.

Group Tactical Objective: Defensive shape and collective movement. Simple attacking solutions.

Technical Objective: Long passing.

Motor Athletic Objective: Quickness.

Duration of Session: 100 minutes

We recommend starting the session with exercises for general mobility to prevent injuries.

| **1. Warm Up** | **4v4 Counter-Movement Small Sided Game** | **20 mins** |

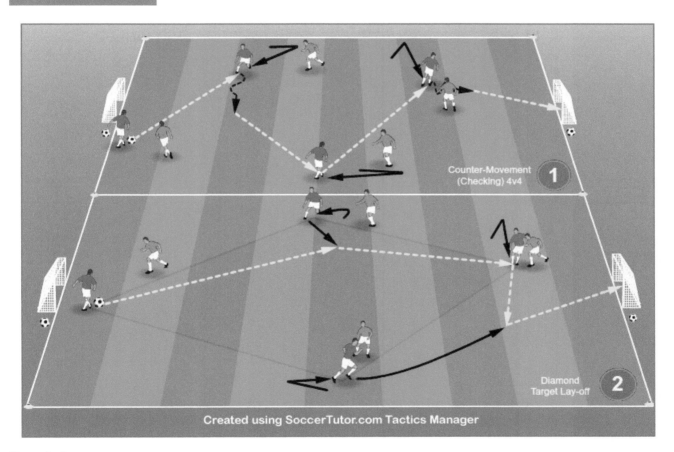

Counter-Movement (Checking) 4v4 **1**

Diamond Target Lay-off **2**

Created using SoccerTutor.com Tactics Manager

Description

Start the warm up with a simple 4v4 game, then add the double goal conditions.

Every goal that is the result of a counter-movement (going long and then short to receive) will be awarded 2 goals.

After 8 minutes switch to play with a diamond shape, with the target player playing only as a wall and laying off the ball to the other 3 players.

Coaching Points

1. Players have to use counter-movements to create space. This is a short movement in one direction followed by the long movement in the opposite direction to receive the ball in space.

2. In Part 2, the target player needs to shield the ball and his lay off needs to be timed well to the supporting run.

2. Conditioning | Coordination & Agility Shooting Race | 10 mins

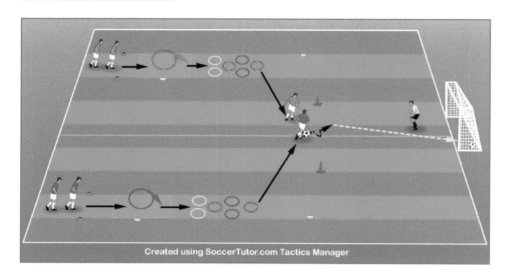

Description

This exercise is a race, so the 2 players start at the same time. Players start with a summersault, skip through the rings and then sprint to the ball, trying to get there first.

The aim is to score.

After 3 minutes, add a pole that the player with the ball must dribble around.

---

3. Game Situation | Creating Space with Counter-Movements in 2v1 Play | 20 mins

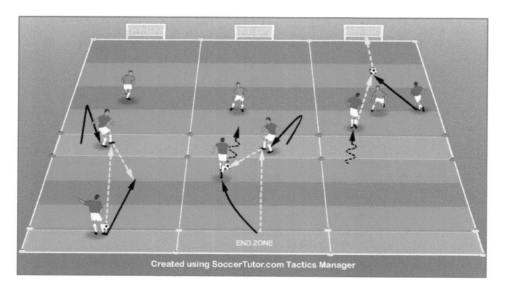

Description

Players are divided into groups of 3.

One of the attacking players (target player) performs a countermovement to create space, receives the ball and lays back to his teammate to start a 2v1 situation.

The objective is to shoot at goal within 5 seconds.

If the defender wins the ball, he can dribble into the end zone to score a goal.

Variations

1. The target player uses one touch to pass back.
2. He uses his head to control the ball and passes back.

4. Tactical Situation Cohesive Movement of the Defensive Unit 20 mins

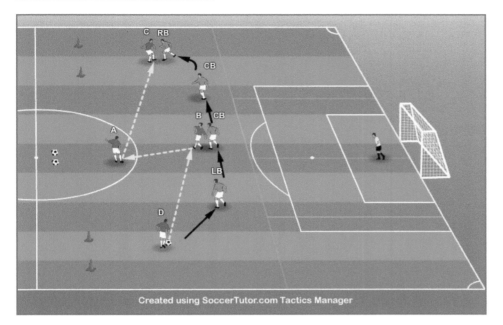

Description

This is a tactical exercise for all the defenders.

The defensive unit is positioned as shown.

Players A, B, C & D move the ball around and the 4 defenders must move as a result adopting the concepts of pressure on the ball and no pressure on the ball (closing down the space or dropping back).

The defenders also provide the proper support when the ball is in wide positions with C and D.

The other players will perform exercises running with the ball.

5. Specific Game Counter-Movement and Attacking Combinations Near the Penalty Area 15 mins

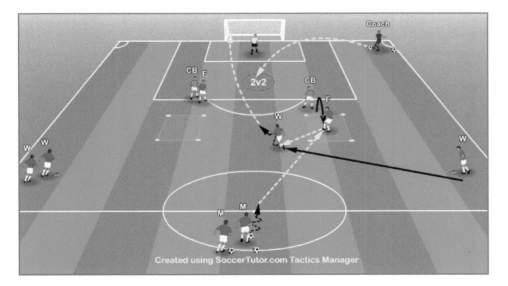
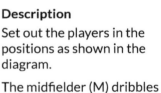

Description

Set out the players in the positions as shown in the diagram.

The midfielder (M) dribbles the ball forwards and one of the strikers makes a counter movement and moves into one of the square zones where the defenders are not allowed to follow.

The forward lays the ball off for one of the wingers (W) who makes a run inside to shoot from distance.

Right after the shot, the coach crosses the ball for a 2v2 between the 2 strikers and the 2 centre backs

| Practice 6   Free Small Sided Game | 20 mins |

TRAINING UNIT FOR WEEK 21 & 22

Individual Tactical Objective: Dribbling and feints.

Technical Objective: Shooting with the weaker foot.

Motor Athletic Objective: Psycho-kinetics and speed endurance.

Duration of Session: 105 minutes

We recommend starting the session with exercises for general mobility to prevent injuries.

1. Warm Up	**4 Colour Passing Sequence**	**10 mins**

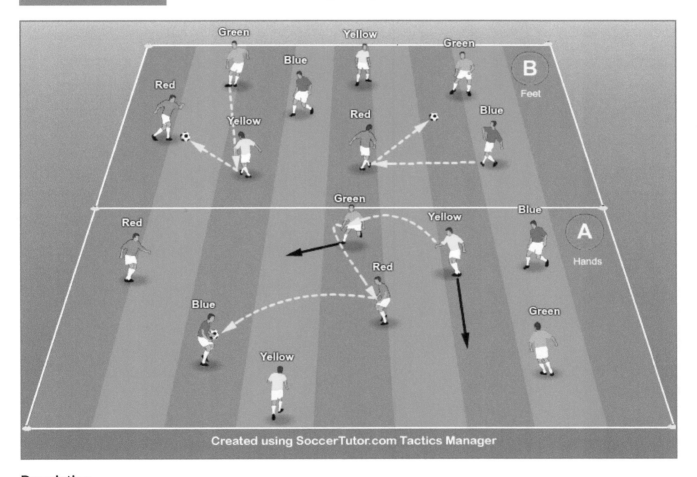

Created using SoccerTutor.com Tactics Manager

Description

Divide the players into 2 groups of 8-10 players. Divide each group into 4 different colours.

We play with hands (A) before progressing to feet with 2 balls (B), with the following rules and variations:

1. Player passes the ball and calls the colour he passes to.
2. Player passes the ball and calls a colour different then the colour he passes the ball to.
3. Player passes the ball and calls the colour that the player receiving the ball must pass to next.
4. Player passes the ball and calls a colour that the player receiving the ball is not allowed to pass to.

2. Conditioning — Pass, Sprint, Turn, Receive and Pass — 15 mins

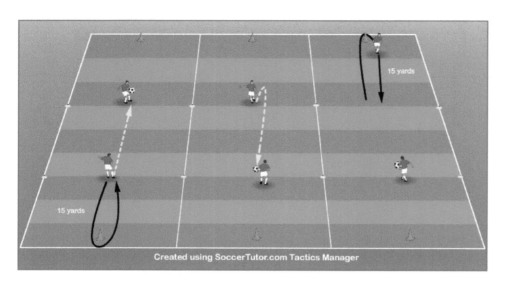

Description

The first player passes the ball to their teammate and runs around the cone behind them (as shown).

The other player juggles the ball as he waits and plays a lofted pass back to the first player. The second player then runs round the cone behind him, while the first player juggles.

Run drill 4 x 3 minutes with 1 minute recovery time in between sets.

3. Technical — Weighted Pass, Agility Poles and Shooting — 20 mins

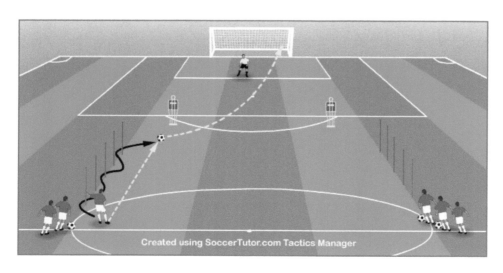

Description

Position 2 lines of 5 poles or cones (50 cm apart) 10 yards outside the penalty area.

The players pass the ball to themselves, run through the poles and shoot at goal. Shoot with the right foot from the left side and the left foot from the right side.

Variations

1. Running backwards.
2. Run from a central position.
3. Run from wide (the flank).
4. Shoot on the half volley with the player using a high throw-in to pass to themselves.

4. Game Situation — Dynamic 1v1 Duels — 20 mins

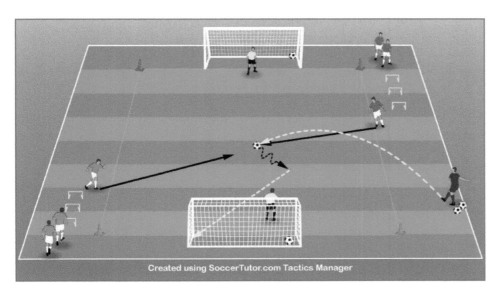

Description

The players jump over the 3 hurdles and race to get to the ball passed into the middle (by the coach) first.

The player who wins the ball shoots at goal. If the goalkeeper saves the shot, he immediately passes to the other player who then attacks the other goal.

Each pair has 3 turns.

Coaching Points

1. Use low hurdles for quick jumps before the sprint to the ball.
2. The players need to be prepared for a transition if the goalkeeper makes a save

5. Specific Game — 6v6 Quick Shooting in a Small Area — 20 mins

Description

In an area 10 x 15 yards, 2 teams of 5 players each try to continuously shoot at goal using quick combination plays.

The goalkeepers can use high balls in order to allow acrobatic shots.

The small area is used to encourage quick shooting.

The remainder of the squad performs exercises dribbling with the left foot.

Practice 6 — Free Small Sided Game — 20 mins

Individual Tactical Objective: Dribbling and feints.

Technical Objective: Shooting and heading.

Motor Athletic Objective: Speed endurance.

Duration of Session: 115 minutes

We recommend starting the session with exercises for general mobility to prevent injuries.

| **1. Warm Up** | Quick Reactions 4v4 Games | **15 mins** |

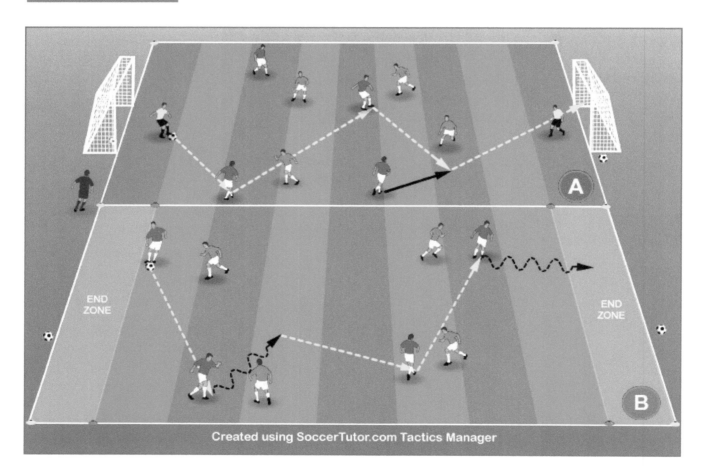

Created using SoccerTutor.com Tactics Manager

Description

Set out 2 pitches (both 15 x 20 yards).

On *FIELD* A, a game of 4v4 is played with goalkeepers. On the coach's call, the teams change the direction of their play by quickly reacting to attack the other goal.

On *FIELD* B, a game of 4v4 is played and a goal is scored by a player dribbling into the end zone.

Coaching Points

1. Field A: The players need to be aware of the changing conditions (quick reactions).
2. Field B: Encourage the players to use feints/moves to beat in 1v1 situations.

2. Conditioning — Sprint, Receive and Passing Triangle — 20 mins

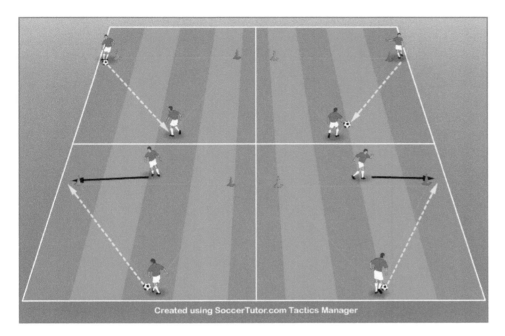

Created using SoccerTutor.com Tactics Manager

Description

The player runs to the red cone, receives the ball and passes it back to their teammate.

They then run to the blue cone and do the same.

Play for 2 minutes at a time, allowing time for recoveryin between.

3. Technical — Shooting from Various Angles — 20 mins

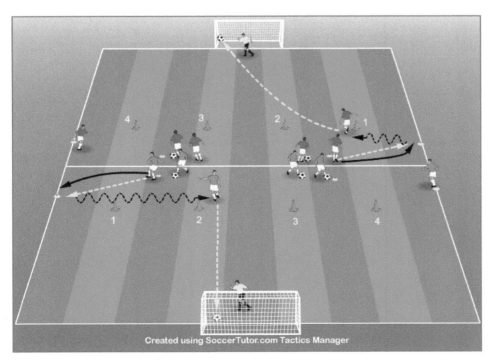

Created using SoccerTutor.com Tactics Manager

Description

Players pass the ball to themselves, collect it and run with the ball to cone 1 and shoot at goal.

The next time, the player shoots from cone 2. After shooting from each of the 4 cones the players change sides and shoot with the other foot.

Variation

When the player reaches the cone, he passes the ball to one side of the cone and runs round the other side and shoots.

4. Game Situation — 3v2 Dynamic Small Sided Game — 20 mins

Created using SoccerTutor.com Tactics Manager

Description

In an area 30 x 15 yards, a game of 3v2 is played.

The team of 3 players has possession at the start and must try to score. If one of the defenders wins the ball, they can then shoot in the other goal without any pressure.

Coaching Points

1. The final ball should be to the player in space without a marker.
2. The defenders need to have good communication and collectively defend their zone and the goal.

5. Specific Game — 5v5 (+5) Heading Support Players in a SSG — 20mins

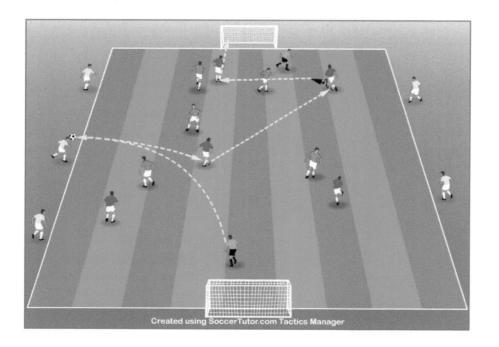

Created using SoccerTutor.com Tactics Manager

Description

We play a 5v5 game with 5 outside support players who can only play with their head.

The goalkeeper must play the ball to the support players for them to head the ball into the field.

Change the support players twice, so each of the 3 teams have an equal share of the roles.

| Practice 6   Free Small Sided Game | 20 mins |

Individual Tactical Objective: Dribbling and feints.

Group Tactical Objective: Ball possession and counter attacking.

Technical Objective: Shooting.

Motor Athletic Objective: Quickness.

Duration of Session: 105 minutes

We recommend starting the session with exercises for general mobility to prevent injuries.

| **1. Warm Up** | 1v1 Play with Feints / Moves to Beat | **15 mins** |

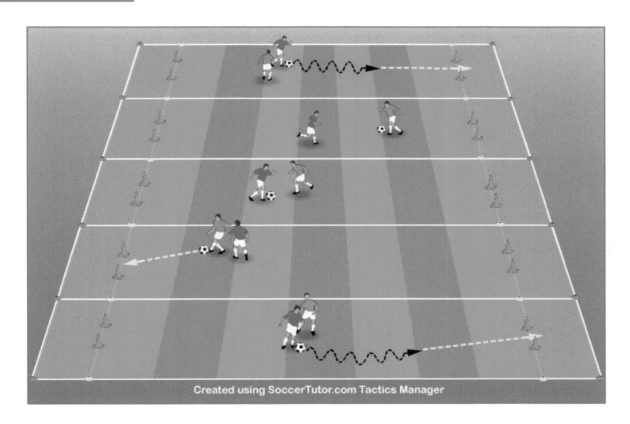

Created using SoccerTutor.com Tactics Manager

Description

Set out 1v1 channels 5 x 10 yards in size. Place 2 small goals (cones) 1 yard wide at the ends.

Players can score by dribbling past their opponent and scoring in the small goal.

If a goal is scored or the ball goes out of play, the defending player becomes the attacker.

Coaching Points

1. The attacking player needs to keep the ball close to their feet using feints and quick changes of direction to get past the defender and score.

2. Players need to have explosive acceleration to continuously beat the defender.

2. Conditioning — Intense Volley Passing Triangle

10 mins

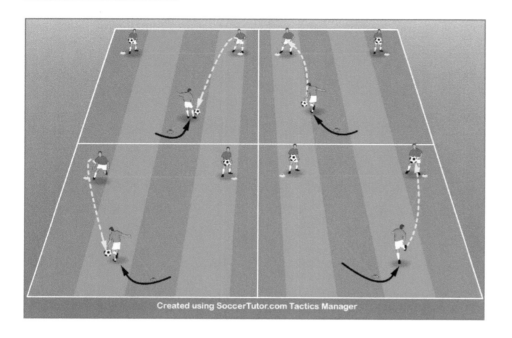

Created using SoccerTutor.com Tactics Manager

Description

3 players form a triangle with 2 acting as servers for the other player.

The red player runs round the cone and volley passes the ball back which is thrown by his teammates.

30 seconds for each type of volley pass:

Inside of foot, instep, half volley with inside of foot, heading, chest and thigh.

---

3. Technical — Shooting from Various Angles (2)

20 mins

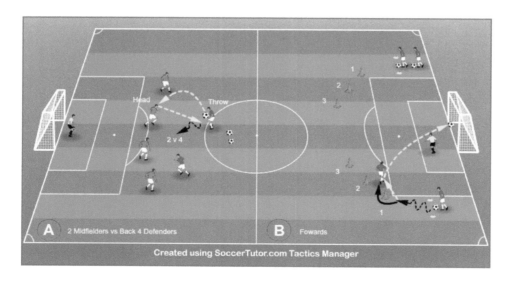

A) 2 Midfielders vs Back 4 Defenders

B) Fowards

Created using SoccerTutor.com Tactics Manager

Description

Midfielders & Defenders
A) We play a 2v4 situation.

One midfielder throws the ball up for a defender who heads the ball back to him.

The midfielder then dribbles forward, trying to play the ball in behind for their teammate to score in this 2v4 situation. The defenders simply try to prevent a goal being scored.

Forwards
B) Every player dribble sto the cone and as shown in the diagram, he turns around it and shoots at goal. All players shoot from all 3 positions and then change sides to shoot with the other foot.

Variation for Forwards
Ask the player to shoot specifically towards the near or far post.

4. Game Situation — 6v6 (+6) Quick Combinations Game — 20 mins

Created using SoccerTutor.com Tactics Manager

Description

2 teams play a 6v6 game with 6 outside support players, who play with the team in possession.

A goal counts as double it if it is from a 1-2 combination with an outside player.

The support players are limited to 1 touch.

Coaching Point

1. Make sure to use the full width of the area and switch the play often to stretch the opposition and fully exploit the numerical advantage with the outside support players.

5. Specific Game — 8v8 Dynamic Transition Game — 20 mins

Created using SoccerTutor.com Tactics Manager

Description

2 teams play an 8v8 game using an area slightly large than half a full pitch.

The blue team can only score by building up play from the back.

The red team are only allowed to score within 12 seconds from the time they win the ball.

After 10 minutes, change the roles of the teams.

Variations

1. Teams play with limited touches
2. The red team can only play forward passes.

Practice 6   Free Small Sided Game — 20 mins

TRAINING UNIT FOR WEEK 23 & 24

Individual Tactical Objective: Dribbling.

Technical Objective: Shooting with a volley using the weaker foot.

Motor Athletic Objective: Speed endurance.

Duration of Session: 120 minutes

We recommend starting the session with exercises for general mobility to prevent injuries.

---

1. Warm Up — Dribbling and Juggling with the Weaker Foot — 20 mins

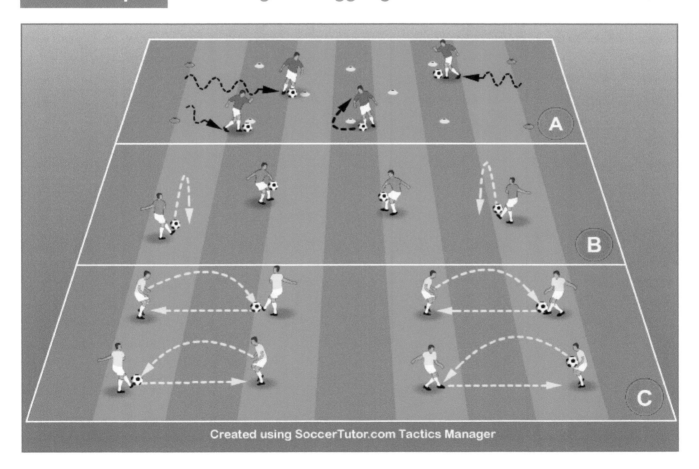

Created using SoccerTutor.com Tactics Manager

Description

We work on all parts of this drill with only the weaker foot:

A) Running with the ball and turning around the cones.

B) Juggling and after 3 touches stop the ball with different parts of the foot: sole, instep, inside, outside.

C) Players are in pairs and control the ball with the chest, using the instep volley, inside of the foot volley and half volley.

2. Conditioning — Quick Passing Competition — 20 mins

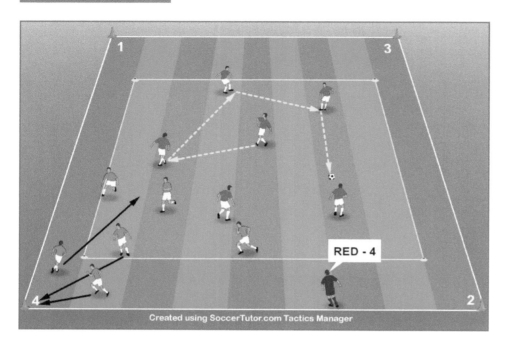

Description

2 teams of 6 players are positioned inside the square.

On the coach's call, the red team runs out of the square towards the cone and then runs back into the square

In the meantime, the blue team must pass the ball inside the square as many times as possible before the red team is back.

Once all the red team is back, the blue team runs out and the process is repeated.

4 repetitions of 2 minutes with a recovery time of 1 and a half minutes in between.

3. Technical — Accurate Shooting on the Volley — 20 mins

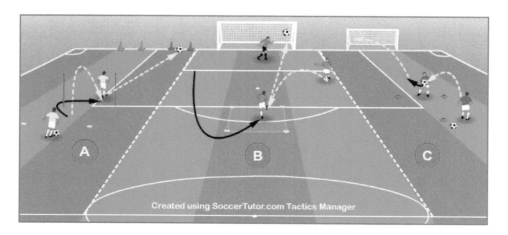

Description

3 exercises to improve shooting with a volley:

A) The player juggles the ball and hits it over 2 poles. He runs around the pole and hits the ball on the volley or after 1 bounce, trying to shoot in one of the small goals.

B) A player starts with his back to goal, runs round the back of the square zone and volleys the ball that has been thrown up by a teammate. The player must hit the ball on a full volley.

C) The player has his back to goal and the ball is thrown up in the air by a teammate. An acrobatic volley is performed to score in the goal.

4. Game Situation   2v2 Agility Game with 4 Goals   20 mins

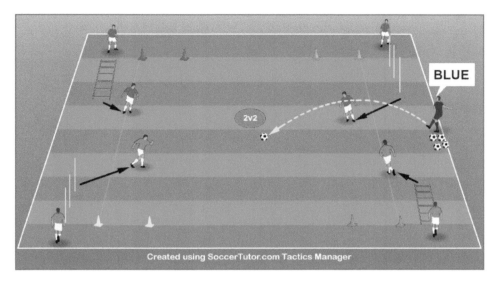

BLUE

2v2

Created using SoccerTutor.com Tactics Manager

Description

After a quick agility circuit (ladder or poles), the players run into the middle to play a 2v2 game.

The team that wins the ball can score in the goal called out by the coach.

If the defending team wins the ball they can score in the opposite goal.

Coaching Points

1. The emphasis with the ladders and the poles is on speed as well as the sprint to the ball.
2. Good vision and awareness is needed to attack the right goal (using a directional first touch).

5. Specific Game   6v6 with 6 Dribble Gates   20 mins

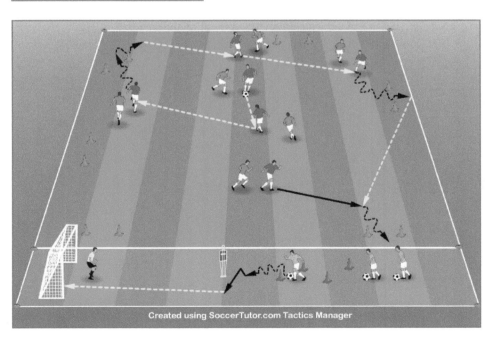

Created using SoccerTutor.com Tactics Manager

Description

In an area 40 x 30 yards, we play a 6v6 games with 6 small cone gates.

A goal is scored by dribbling through the cones, but a player canno score in the same goal twice.

The players not involved perform a series of dribbling and feints on a circuit with final shooting.

Every 5 minutes a new team is called to play.

Practice 6   Free Small Sided Game   20 mins

Individual Tactical Objective: Dribbling and feints.

Technical Objective: Shooting and receiving the ball.

Motor Athletic Objective: Psycho-kinetics and speed endurance.

Duration of Session: 110 minutes

We recommend starting the session with exercises for general mobility to prevent injuries.

| **1. Warm Up** | **4 Colours Awareness Passing Sequence** | **10 mins** |

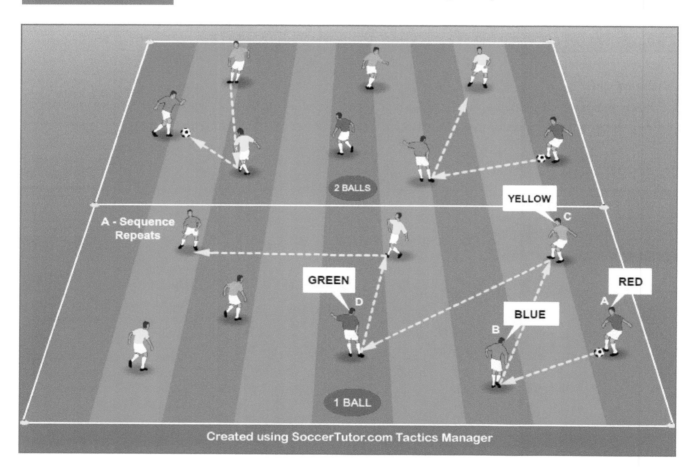

Created using SoccerTutor.com Tactics Manager

Description

Divide the players into 2 groups of 8-10 players and divide each group into 4 colours. The players pass the ball around with these different rules:

1. The player passes the ball and calls out the colour he is passing to.
2. The second player passes the ball and calls out a colour different to the one he passes to.
3. The third player passes the ball and calls out a colour that the receiving player must pass to.
4. The fourth player passes the ball and calls out a colour that the receiving player cannot pass to.

Variation

Use 2 balls as shown in the example at the top of the diagram.

2. Conditioning   One-Two and Shoot / 20 Yard Sprints   20 mins

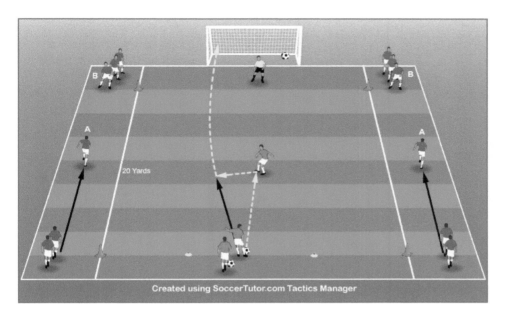

Description

Set up the drill as shown the diagram. The red players play a 1-2 and try to score as many goals as possible while the blue players perform a series of 20 yard sprints.

The blue players must complete 4 sprints of 20 yards each.

Player A sprints towards B who starts the sprint as soon as he is tagged by A.

3. Technical   Receiving and Shooting in Front of Goal   20 mins

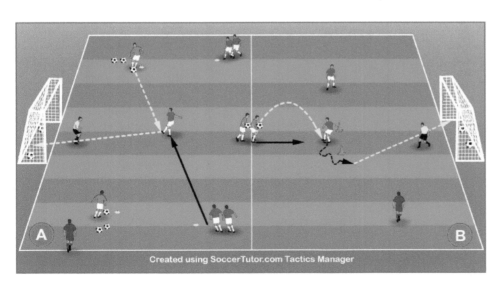

Description

A) The players start out wide and make a diagonal run to the middle, right in front of goal.

The 2 red players act as servers and play the ball in timed for the run to shoot quickly at goal.

The ball is received on the ground, in mid air and in the air.

B) The player receives the ball with his back to the goal and he must receive and control the ball around the cone before shooting. The ball is received on the ground, in mid air and in the air.

4. Game Situation — 1v1 Dribbling and Shooting Duel — 20 mins

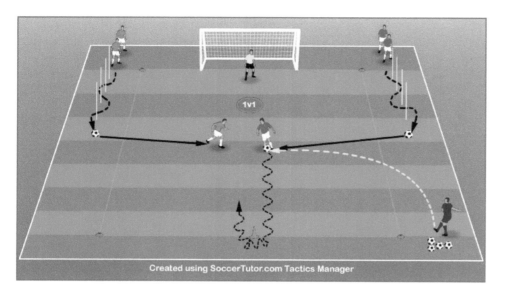

Description

2 players dribble the ball around the poles and at the end they leave the ball and sprint inside to win the ball played in by the coach.

The first player to the ball must dribble to the cone outside the area and turn around it. The other player must run and touch a cone beside the goal.

The defender then moves quickly to apply pressure to the player with the ball as he dribbles forwards.

The attacker tries to work space to shoot by beating the defender with a dribbling move (feint).

5. Specific Game — Playing in Behind with 6 Dribble Gates — 20mins

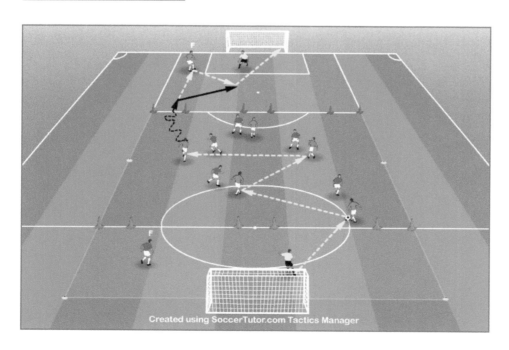

Description

In the area shown, we have 3 goals at the edge of the box and 3 goals on the halfway line.

Players must dribble through the goals. Once they achieve this, they play a 1-2 with the forward (F) and shoot on goal with their stronger foot.

Progress to this from using a stationary ball and shooting with the weaker foot.

Practice 6 · Free Small Sided Game — 20 mins

Individual Tactical Objective: Dribbling and feints.

Group Tactical Objective: Overlapping, crossing and attacking interchanges.

Technical Objective: Shooting.

Motor Athletic Objective: Quickness.

Duration of Session: 110 minutes

We recommend starting the session with exercises for general mobility to prevent injuries.

| 1. Warm Up | Dribbling and Feints in Pairs | 20 mins |

Created using SoccerTutor.com Tactics Manager

Description

In an area 20 x 20 yards, the players dribble around in pairs with 1 ball between them.

On the coach's call, the player with the ball dribbles towards his teammate who acts as passive defender and performs various types of feints.

Once the player goes past their teammate, they pass the ball back to them and the same is repeated by the other player.

After 10 minutes, the defenders become active.

Coaching Points

1. Get the players to use various different feints/moves to beat.
2. Start with the defenders being inactive, then half active and finishing with fully active.

2. Conditioning   Pass and Move Sequence with 3 Players (2)   10 mins

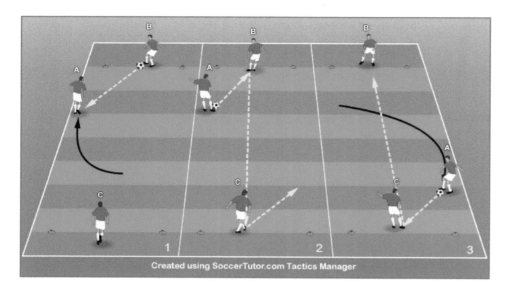

Description

3 players play a simple passing and receiving practice with 1 player in the middle working hard.

The player in the middle stays there for 30 seconds. Player B passes to A,

Player A passes back to B. Player B passes to C and A moves to receive off C and the sequence continues.

3. Technical   Awareness & Changing Direction with the Ball   15 mins

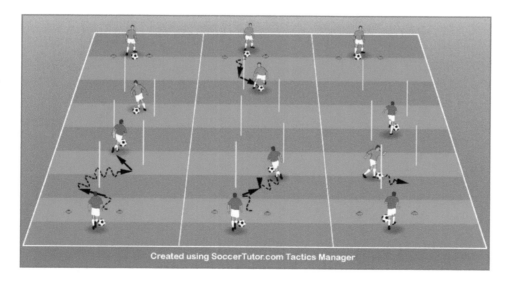

Description

Place 2 lines of 5 poles in a zig zag pattern for a total distance of 7-10 yards.

Players dribble around the poles using various feints:

1. Step over.
2. Double step over.
3. Maradona move.
4. Any other feints.

Progression

Introduce a time limit to increase the intensity and quickness of play.

Coaching Points

1. Changes of direction through the poles should be with small steps and bended knees.
2. The tempo should be quick with players using both feet in all parts.

4. Game Situation — Collective Movements & Combinations with Overlapping Run, Crossing & Finishing — 25 mins

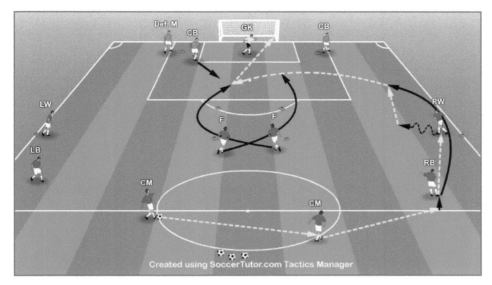

Description

Place all the players in their correct positions, except for the red centre backs.

The practice starts with one of the centre midfielders with the ball who passes to the opposite full back.

The full back plays the ball to the winger and makes an overlapping run to receive high up on the flank.

The winger receives the ball, dribbles inside and passes the ball to the overlapping full back who crosses the ball. At the time of the cross, the forwards must make criss-crossing runs and 1 centre back moves from their cone to mark one of the forwards.

Progression

Introduce another centre back to create a 2v2 in the penalty area.

5. Specific Game — 6v6 Crossing & Finishing 5 Zone Game — 20 mins

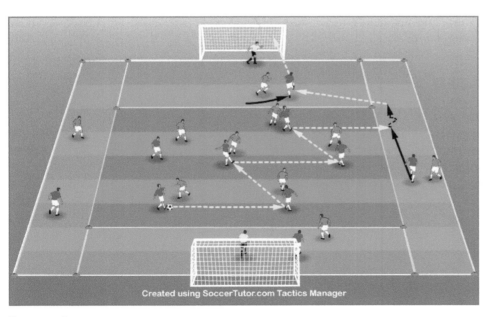

Description

We have a 5 zone game, with 2 attacking zones and 2 side zones. In the central zone we have a 6v6. In the side zones, we have 1 player from each team and in the attacking zones we have 1 attacker.

We start play in the central zone and after a determined number of passes the ball is played to a side player who can cross without any pressure and cross the ball into the attacking zone for their teammate to score.

Change the roles often.

Progression

Introduce a defender in the attacking zone to create a fully active 1v1 situation for the cross (as shown in the diagram).

Practice 6   Free Small Sided Game   **20 mins**

TRAINING UNIT FOR WEEK 25 & 26

Individual Tactical Objective: Shielding of the ball.

Technical Objective: Receiving.

Motor Athletic Objective: Conditional abilities in situation.

Duration of Session: 105 minutes

We recommend starting the session with exercises for general mobility to prevent injuries.

1. Warm Up — Juggling, Control and Short Bursts of Dribbling — 20 mins

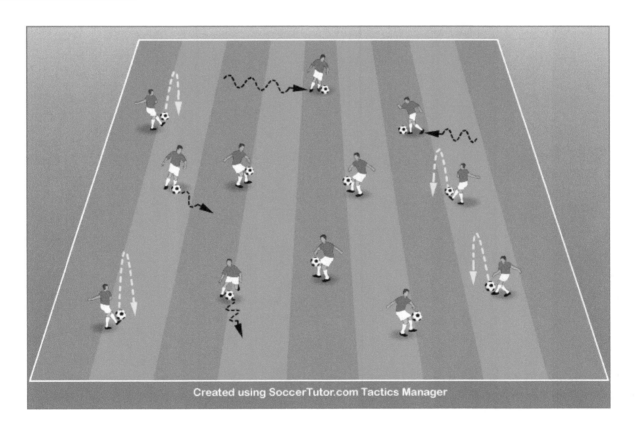

Created using SoccerTutor.com Tactics Manager

Description

Each player has a ball and they are all juggling.

After a few juggles, the players kick the ball up in the air and then receive and control the ball with different parts of the foot: inside, outside and instep of foot, with the thigh, chest and with the head.

After each time the players receive the ball, they must run with the ball over a short distance.

Coaching Points

1. The players should use soft touches to keep close control of the ball.
2. Directional touches with all parts of the feet should be used in this warm up.

2. Conditioning Sprinting & Agility with Crossing & Heading   15 mins

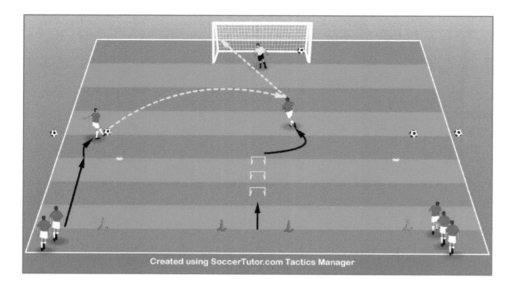

Description

This is a specific exercise for the wingers and full backs.

The wingers and full backs sprint for 20 yards, stop at the cone and re-start the run towards the ball and cross into the middle.

The rest of the players jump over the 3 hurdles performing a heading gesture and then move to head the ball from the cross.

3. Technical Receiving with Back to Goal and Shooting   15 mins

Description

We run this practice from both sides. Player A passes to B and takes his place.

Player B performs a counter-movement, receives the ball and shoots.

Use various types of receiving the ball and make it a competition.

Coaching Points

1. The player should receive the ball moving towards the ball and on the half turn.
2. A directional first touch should push the ball out in front of him to be able to shoot with the second touch.

4. Game Situation — Receiving with Back to Goal Dynamic 1v1 Duels

25 mins

Description

Set up pitches with a small goal and an end zone for 1v1 games.

The attacker receives the ball and must shield it for 5 seconds with from the pressure of the defender.

If he is successful in protecting the ball he can shoot in the goal.

If the defender wins the ball he can score by dribbling into the end zone.

Coaching Points

1. The correct body shape is required to shield the ball, making sure their body is a barrier between the opponent and the ball.
2. Explosive acceleration is needed to beat the defender and score in the goal.

5. Specific Game — 5v5 'Pass to the Captain' Game

20 mins

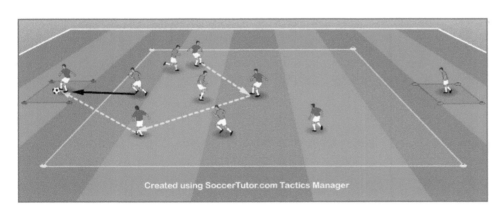

Description

In an area 20 x 20 yards we have a 5v5 game with each team having a player in a zone outside.

The objective of the attacking team is to pass the ball to the captain who is standing in a zone 5 x 5 yards at least 5 yards away from the main square.

To score a point the captain must receive the ball and shield it for 5 seconds from the pressure of one opponent who is allowed to leave the main square to win the ball.

Practice 6   Free Small Sided Game

20 mins

Individual Tactical Objective: Shielding the ball.

Technical Objective: Receiving.

Motor Athletic Objective: Conditional abilities in game situations.

Duration of Session: 105 minutes

We recommend starting the session with exercises for general mobility to prevent injuries.

| 1. Warm Up | Awareness & Receiving with the Chest | 15 mins |

Created using SoccerTutor.com Tactics Manager

Description

3 teams move freely around the area and pass the 3 balls using their hands with the only rule to pass the ball to a different colour to themselves.

When the ball is thrown in the air, the player must receive the ball with their chest and then catch it with their hands.

Variations

1. Change the method of receiving the ball.
2. Have the whole game performed while juggling.

2. Conditioning   RWTB & 1-2 Combinations Passing Circle   **15 mins**

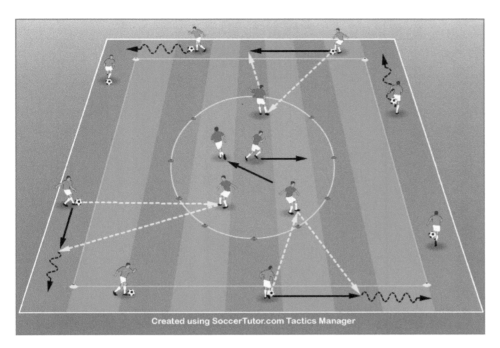

Created using SoccerTutor.com Tactics Manager

Description

The centre midfielders are inside the circle and are always moving and must play 1-2 combinations with the other players who run with the ball around the outside square.

Each outside player runs in a 30 yard circuit outside the circle with the ball at maximum speed.

3. Technical   Passing and Receiving with an Obstacle   **20 mins**

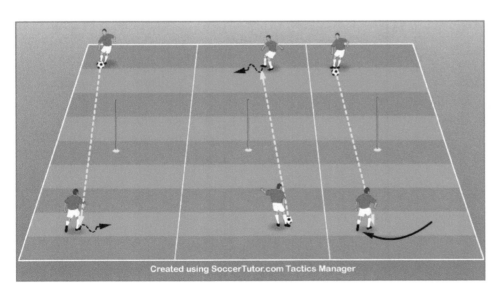

Created using SoccerTutor.com Tactics Manager

Description

As shown in the diagram, the players are facing each other with a pole in between to act as an obstacle.

Player A passes to B with the inside of the foot.

Player B receives with his left foot and directs the ball to his right foot to pass back to A.

Variations

1. Pass with the right foot and receive with the left foot.
2. Pass with the left foot and receive with the right.
3. Pass with the right foot and receive with the outside of the left foot (and vice-versa).

4. Game Situation — 2v1 Play with Shielding of the Ball — 15 mins

Created using SoccerTutor.com Tactics Manager

Description

Set up 15 x 10 yard 2v1 zones.

The first player passes the ball to his teammate (who performs a counter-movement and must shield the ball from the pressure of the defender).

After making the pass, the first player must run in a figure of eight shape (as shown) and at the end of it he can support his teammate to play a 2v1 game.

Coaching Points

1. The correct body shape is required to shield the ball, making sure their body is a barrier between the opponent and the ball.

2. The supporting run needs to be at the right angle and timed well.

5. Specific Game — Quick Passing with Outside Runners — 20 mins

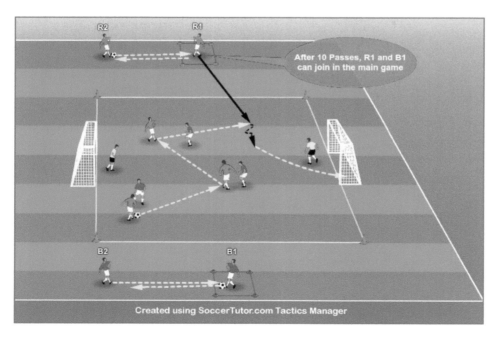

After 10 Passes, R1 and B1 can join in the main game

Created using SoccerTutor.com Tactics Manager

Description

We play a 3v3 in an area 40 x 30 yards.

Outside of this area, mark out two 5 x 5 zones.

B1 & B2/ R1 & R2 must pass and receive the ball correctly 10 times with both the right and left foot.

At the end of these 10 passes they can join the game.

Practice 6   Free Small Sided Game — 20 mins

Individual Tactical Objective: Shielding the ball.

Group Tactical Objective: Movements of centre midfielders when not in possession.

Technical Objective: Receiving and shooting.

Motor Athletic Objective: Quickness.

Duration of Session: 105 minutes

We recommend starting the session with exercises for general mobility to prevent injuries.

| 1. Warm Up | RWTB and Shielding – 'Kick the Ball Out' | 20 mins |

Outside Juggling Zone

Created using SoccerTutor.com Tactics Manager

Description

In this warm up we have 10 players playing against each other with every player dribbling a ball.

On the coach's call, the players must shield their own ball and try to kick their opponent's balls out of the square.

The last 3 players left get a point. The players eliminated wait for the next game by juggling.

Coaching Points

1. The players need to use soft touches to keep close control of the ball at all times.
2. Good awareness is key, making sure to change direction with the ball when under pressure to avoid being tackled and when tackling others (to prevent anyone else approaching at the same time).

2. Conditioning — Sprint, Turn and Volley — 10 mins

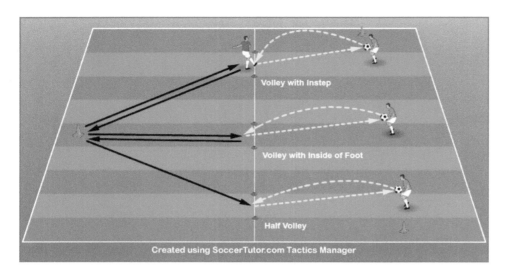

Description

1 player works with 3 servers and starts on the cone. He sprints to the first station, back to the cone, to the 2nd cone, back and finally to the 3rd.

At each station they perform different passes:

1. Volley with the instep.
2. Volley with inside of the foot
3. Half volley.

---

3. Technical — Receiving and Shooting on the Edge of the Box — 15 mins

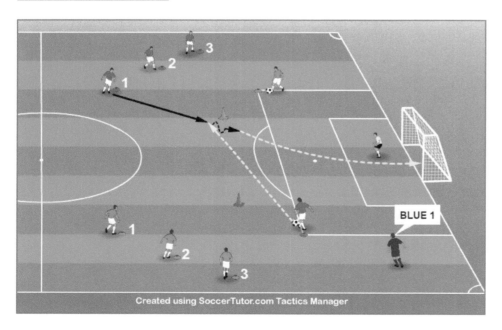

Description

Players are placed in 3 different positions (1 , 2 & 3).

The coach calls out a player's number and that player must sprint towards the cone to receive the pass from their teammate.

The first touch should be in the direction of the goal before shooting. The 3 different positions reflect three different angles for receiving the ball.

Variations

1. Ball passed on the ground (receiving with the inside/outside of the foot.
2. Chip pass and receive with ball bouncing.
3. Aerial pass and receive the ball with the chest.

4. Game Situation — Movements of the Centre Midfielders when Not in Possession of the Ball — 20 mins

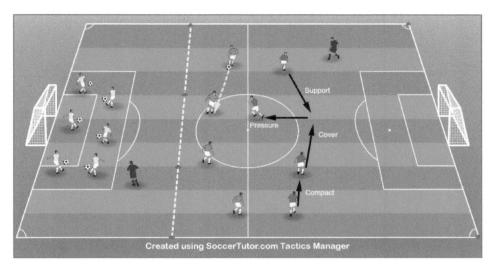

Description

Based on the 4-4-2 formation, position 4 centre midfielders on the pitch as shown. In front of them, 4 players pass the ball to each other. The 4 midfielders focus on movements applying pressure to the player in possession of the ball and covering/supporting.

The other players not involved in the activity work on juggling the ball with various themes within the penalty area.

Variation

Change the position of the 4 opponents (in defensive half or attacking half and change the tactical positioning or formation of the opponents.

5. Specific Game — Receiving from Accurate Long Passing and Crossing — 20 mins

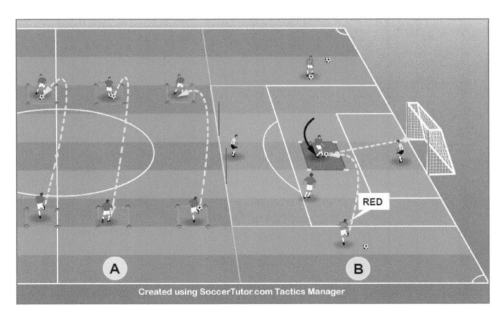

Description

EXERCISE A
The players stand inside small squares and they must pass and receive 40 times within the squares.

EXERCISE B
These players are involved in a game of crossing and finishing.

The wide players cross into the square zone in the middle of the penalty area for their teammate to finish

The attacker must receive inside the square and score in the goal with the colour called out by the crosser.

Practice 6 — Free Small Sided Game — 20 mins

TRAINING UNIT FOR WEEK 27 & 28

Individual Tactical Objective: Shielding of the ball.

Technical Objective: Receiving and passing.

Motor Athletic Objective: Conditional abilities in game situations.

Duration of Session: 110 minutes

We recommend starting the session with exercises for general mobility to prevent injuries.

| 1. Warm Up | Pass and Move Sequence with 3 Players (3) | **15 mins** |

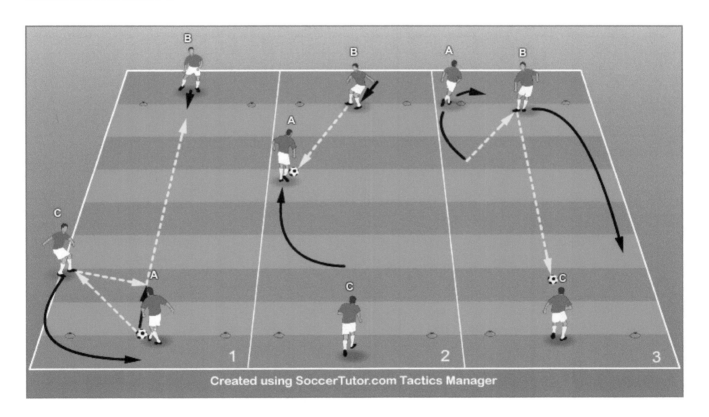

Description

3 players are 15 yards apart and pass the ball using 2 touches, focusing on the proper technique of receiving the ball.

Player A plays a 1-2 combination with Player C and then passes to Player B. Player C takes A's position as Player A moves to play a 1-2 combination with Player B. Player B passes to C and the sequence continues.

Variations

1. Passing on the ground.
2. Aerial passing (increase the distance to 30 yards).
3. Keep the ball up by juggling the whole time.

2. Conditioning — 1v1 Quick Reaction Sprints to the Ball — 15 mins

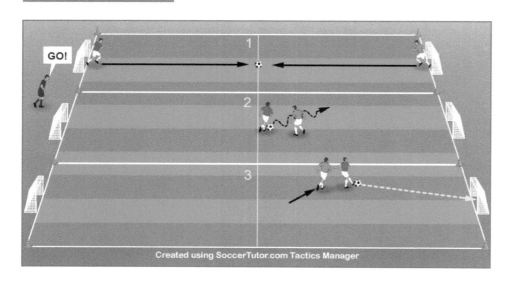

Description

At the coach's call, the 2 players sprint 15 yards to get to the ball first and score starting from the following positions:

1. Laying on the ground on their back.
2. Laying on the ground on their front.
3. Sitting position.
4. Jumping on the spot

3. Technical — Receiving with Good Awareness and the Correct Body Shape — 20 mins

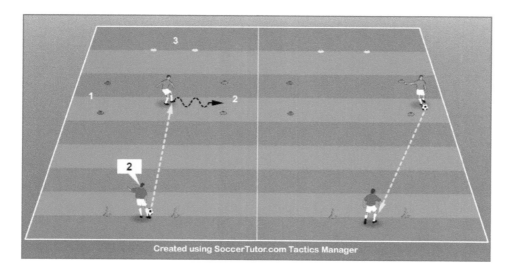

Description

The red player stands in the middle of the field with 3 small cone goals.

The blue player passes the ball in and calls out a number.

The red player must take a directional first touch towards the cones called out, then pass the ball back (as shown).

The player works for 1.5 minutes before switching roles with the server.

Variations

1. Receive the ball on the ground.
2. Receive the ball in mid air.
3. Receive ball in the air.
4. Use all parts of the body to control the ball

4. Game Situation — 1v1 Receiving and Shielding the Ball — 20 mins

Description

The attacking player stands in the centre of the area with his back to the defender. The yellow player passes the ball and calls out the colour of a goal. The attacker must try to score in the opposite goal to the one called out.

The attacker must take a directional first touch and shield the ball for 5 seconds. At the same time the defender closes in on the attacker.

Coaching Points

1. To shield the ball for 5 seconds, the player must make their body a barrier between the defender and the ball.

2. When receiving the ball, the player should take a directional first touch towards the opposite goal that is called out.

5. Specific Game — 8v8 Passing Box 3 Zone Game — 20 mins

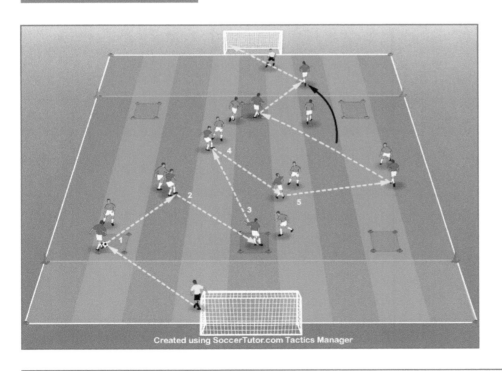

Description

We have a 9v9 game with 3 zones. Position 6 square zones with an area of 2 x 2 yards near each attacking zone.

After completing 5 passes, the team in possession can pass the ball into one of the boxes.

If a player receives correctly in the box, he can pass the ball to a teammate who has made a run into the attacking zone who can shot without pressure.

Practice 6   Free Small Sided Game — 20 mins

Individual Tactical Objective: Positioning to defend the goal.

Technical Objective: Heading.

Motor Athletic Objective: Conditional abilities in game situations.

Duration of Session: 115 minutes

We recommend starting the session with exercises for general mobility to prevent injuries.

| 1. Warm Up | Throw-ins and Headers Game | 20 mins |

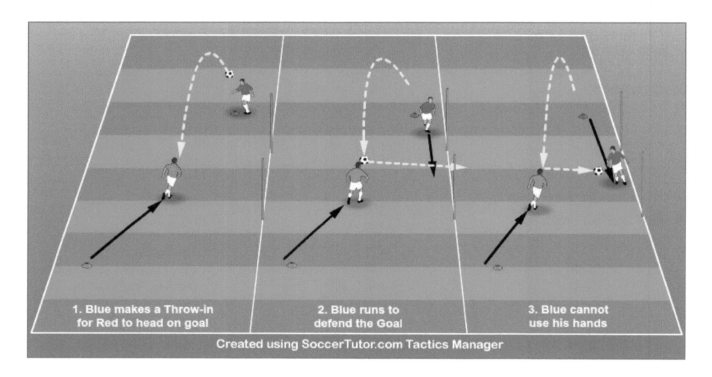

1. Blue makes a Throw-in for Red to head on goal
2. Blue runs to defend the Goal
3. Blue cannot use his hands

Created using SoccerTutor.com Tactics Manager

Description

The blue player throws-in for the blue player and positions himself to defend the goal without using his hands.

The red player heads the ball at goal. The blue player quickly moves to defend the goal and tries to save without using his hands.

The exercise should be run as a competition between the players (a point for a goal and a point for a save).

Coaching Points

1. There should be sufficient height on the throw to allow the player to move across and be the goalkeeper.
2. The timing of the run forward to meet the ball and head with power is the key to good execution.

2. Conditioning | Applying Quick Pressure in a 3 Zone Game | 15 mins

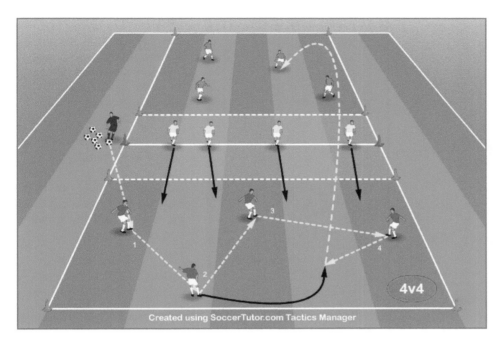

Description

In this practice we have 3 teams of 4 and 3 zones.

The blue team must make 4 passes before making a long pass to the red team.

The yellow team applies pressure to the team in possession. If they win the ball, the team who lost possession become the defending team and must apply pressure to the other team once the long pass has been made.

3. Technical | Heading on the Run with Mini Goals | 20 mins

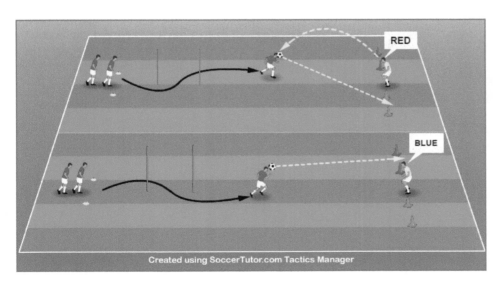

Description

In 2 teams, up to 8 players play in 2 different fields. In each area we have 2 mini goals of different colours.

The blue players run through the 2 poles and sprint forwards.

The yellow players throw the ball up and call out a colour of one of the 2 goals.

The blue player heads the ball towards the coloured goal called out by their teammate.

Coaching Points

1. The timing of the throw to the run is important so the player does not have to slow down or stop before heading the ball.

2. The player needs quick reactions and awareness to head into the right goal.

4. Game Situation — 3v3 Attacking / Defending Crosses — 15 mins

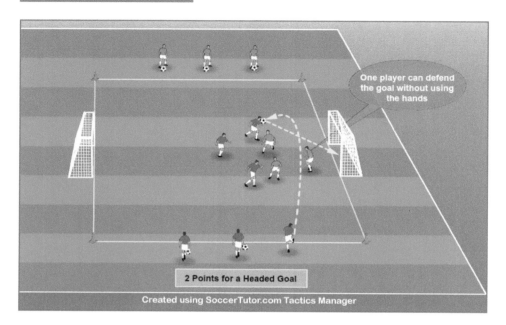

One player can defend the goal without using the hands

2 Points for a Headed Goal

Created using SoccerTutor.com Tactics Manager

Description

We play with 2 teams of 6 players. There are 3 players positioned on each side to cross the ball for their 3 teammates in the middle to score.

The teams alternate crossing the ball. A goal scored with the head counts as double. 1 player per team can defend the goal but they are not allowed to use their hands.

Coaching Points

1. The cross and the run need to be well coordinated.

2. When under pressure from a defender, the attacker needs to check away/change direction to create space.

5. Specific Game — 5v5 (+4) Headed Finishing Game — 20 mins

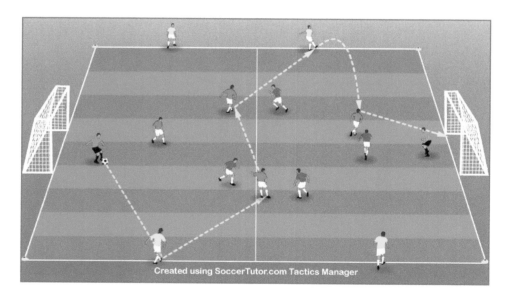

Created using SoccerTutor.com Tactics Manager

Description

Set up a long and narrow pitch.

We play a 5v5 game with 4 neutral support players at the sides who play with the team in possession.

Goals can only be scored with a header from a neutral support player's cross.

Coaching Points

1. The team in possession should make sure to use the full width by switching play (making the most of their numerical advantage by stretching the opposition).

2. The timing of the cross and the run need to be coordinated.

Practice 6   Free Small Sided Game   20 mins

SESSION 42

Group Tactical Objective: Collective movements when not in possession of the ball.

Technical Objective: Heading.

Motor Athletic Objective: Quickness.

Duration of Session: 110 minutes

We recommend starting the session with exercises for general mobility to prevent injuries.

| 1. Warm Up | 2v2 Football Tennis Tournament | 20 mins |

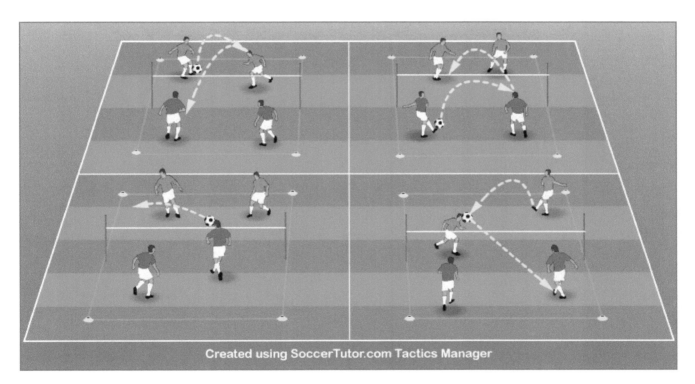

Created using SoccerTutor.com Tactics Manager

Description

Set up various mini pitches and play football tennis with the following rules:

1. A point can only be won with a headed finish.
2. Only allow 3 touches per team and the ball can only bounce once.
3. A player must play the ball to his teammate before playing the ball back over the net.

Coaching Points

1. The players should try to use all parts of the foot, thigh, chest and head to maximise control of the ball.
2. The pass to the teammate should have good height for the headed finishes.

2. Conditioning — Speed, Agility & Coordination Circuit — 10 mins

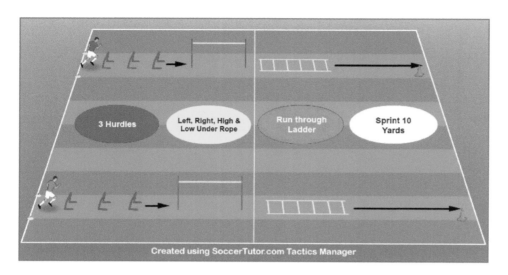

Description

First the players jump over 3 low hurdles, then they go under the rope moving left and right of it and by lowering and raising their body.

The circuit finishes with a speed ladder and a 10 yard sprint.

3. Technical — Headed Juggling Sequence with 3 Players — 15 mins

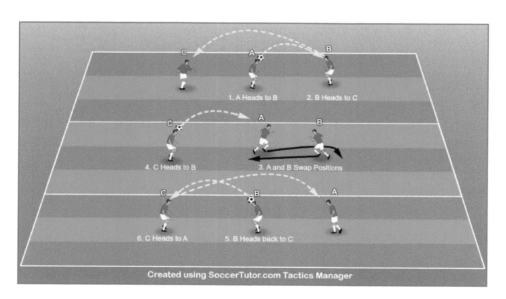

Description

3 players work on their heading technique using 1 or 2 touches in this juggling exercise.

The players try to keep the ball in the air passing it only with their heads.

Player A heads to B and B heads to C. Player B then changes position with A.

Player C heads to B and B returns the ball to C who heads to A.

4. Game Situation — Position Specific Team Shape Shadow Play — 20 mins

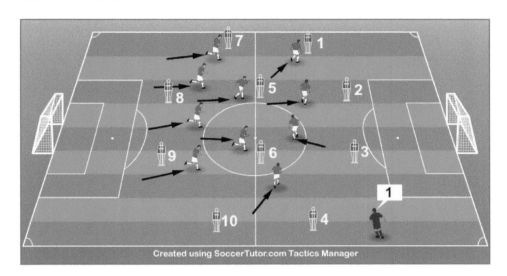

Description

Set the team out according to the system played (i.e. 4-4-2) and place 11 flags or mannequins and number them all.

The coach calls out a number which relates to an opposition player. The players move and shift, adjusting the team shape pretending that player has possession of the ball.

Coaching Points

1. The players need to use collective movements, making sure to prevent the passing angles to the other players (mannequins or flags).

2. This practice should be done at a high intensity to replicate the movements during a game.

5. Specific Game — Headed Finishing with Support Players — 20 mins

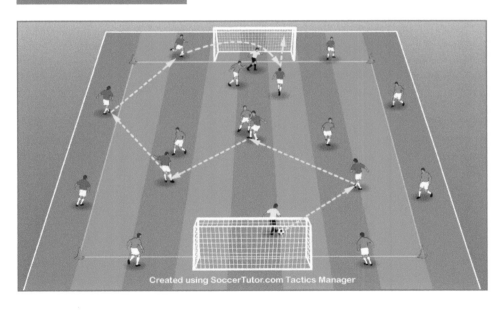

Description

A game is played with each team having 4 players inside the area and 4 additional players on the outside (2 on the side and 2 either side of the goal).

The teams aim to use the support players who can pass the ball to each other as well.

The game is played first with the hands, then hands and feet and finally only with feet.

The goals scored with a header count as double.

Coaching Points

1. The cross and the run need to be well coordinated.

2. When under pressure from a defender, the attacker needs to check away/change direction to create space.

Practice 6 — Free Small Sided Game — 20 mins

TRAINING UNIT FOR WEEK 29 & 30

Individual Tactical Objective: Positioning to defend the goal.

Technical Objective: Heading.

Motor Athletic Objective: Conditional abilities in game situations.

Duration of Session: 110 minutes

We recommend starting the session with exercises for general mobility to prevent injuries.

| **1. Warm Up** | Defending the Goal in a 1v1 | **20 mins** |

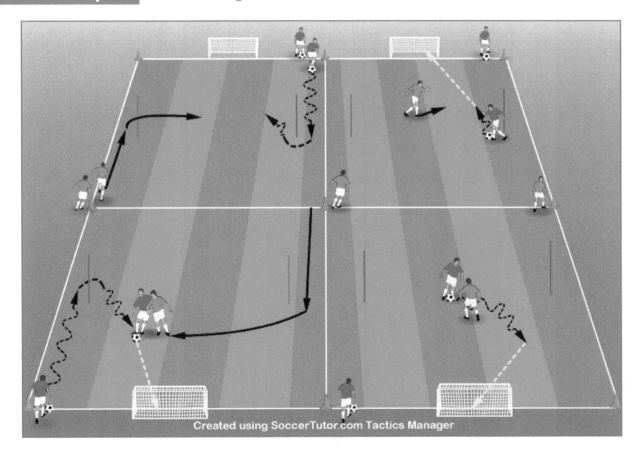

Created using SoccerTutor.com Tactics Manager

Description
Set out many mini fields for 1v1 games. As shown in the diagram, the blue player (attacker) dribbles the ball to the pole and turns around it before trying to shoot at goal.

The red player (defender) runs around the pole and quickly moves to defend the goal and prevent the attacker from scoring. Change roles halfway through and the team that scores the most goals wins.

Coaching Points
1. In the movement around the pole, the players need to keep low to create a sharp change of direction, slowing down before accelerating.
2. The players should attack the space in behind the defender using various feints/moves to beat.

2. Conditioning — Strengthening Exercises & Possession Game   10 mins

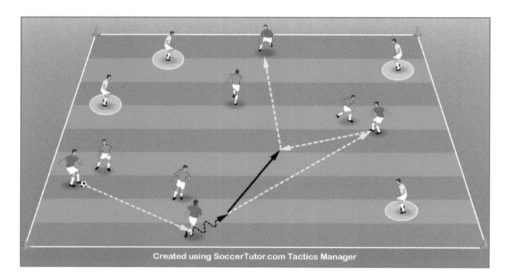

Description

The group is divided into 3 teams. 2 teams play a possession game, while the third team performs strengthening exercises (squats, push-ups, sit-ups).

After 10 repetitions, the team performing the strengthening exercises move to try and win possession of the ball.

3. Technical — Headed Juggling Sequence with 4 Players   20 mins

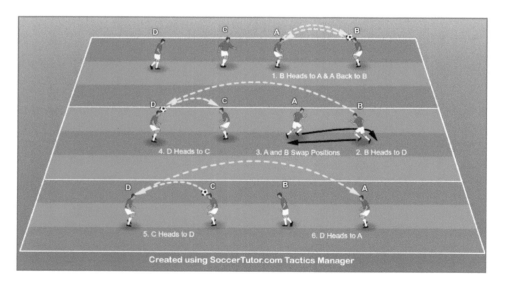

Description

In this headed juggling exercise, 4 players stand in a line.

Player B heads to A, Player A heads back to B. Player B heads to D.

Player D heads to C and C heads back to D. Finally, D heads to A who in the meantime has changed positions with B.

Coaching Points

1. Players need to be able to use different types of headers; short, medium and long.

2. There should be good height on the headers to make it easier for their teammate to make the next header and keep the 'rally' going.

4. Game Situation — 2v1 with Agility Circuit & Headed Pass — 20 mins

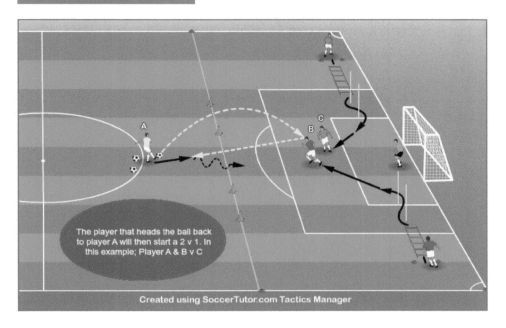

The player that heads the ball back to player A will then start a 2 v 1. In this example; Player A & B v C

Created using SoccerTutor.com Tactics Manager

Description

We use the area shown with a large goal at one end and 2 small goals at the other end.

Player A starts from outside the area and plays a long ball for players B and C.

Player B and player C must first perform an athletic exercise (speed ladder and run through the poles), then try to attack the ball and head it back to player A.

The player who arrives first to the ball and heads it back to A plays with him in a 2v1 situation trying to score in the large goal.

The other player (C in the diagram) defends and if he wins the ball, he can score in one of the 2 small goals.

5. Specific Game — Four Colour Heading Game — 20 mins

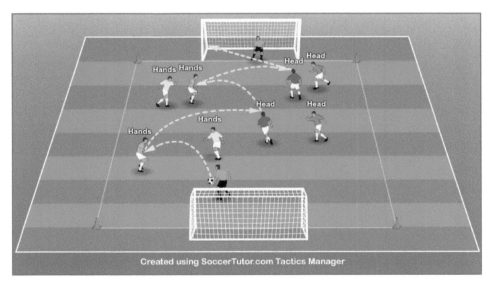

Created using SoccerTutor.com Tactics Manager

Description

We play a 6v6 with each team made up of 2 colours. The blues and oranges play together and the reds and yellows play together.

One colour use just their hands and the other colour just their heads.

A goal can only be scored with a header.

Practice 6 — Free Small Sided Game — 20 mins

SESSION 44

Individual Tactical Objective: Positioning to defend the goal.

Technical Objective: Heading.

Motor Athletic Objective: Conditional abilities in situation.

Duration of Session: 110 minutes

We recommend starting the session with exercises for general mobility to prevent injuries.

| 1. Warm Up | Defending the Goal Using Good Body Shape | 20 mins |

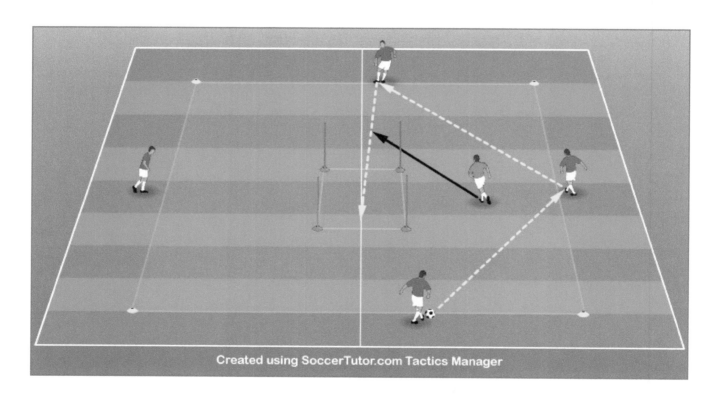

Created using SoccerTutor.com Tactics Manager

Description

We mark out a square with a 4 sided goal in the middle.

4 players stand on the sides of the box and pass the ball to each other with the objective to score in one of the 4 sides of the goal in the middle.

The defender must use the correct body shape and position himself to defend the goal, moving whenever the players make a pass.

Coaching Points

1. The angle of the movement and the correct body shape are needed for the defender to be able to block the shooting path.

2. The blue players should move the ball quickly, using 1 touch when possible.

2. Conditioning — Motor Exercise with 2v1 Duel — 10 mins

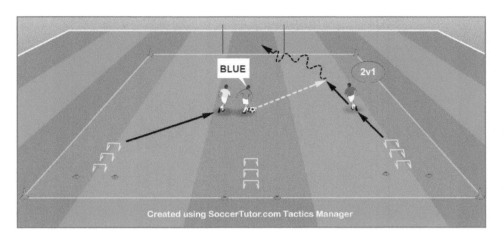

Description

3 players with different colours jump over 3 hurdles and sprint 15 yards towards the ball.

The first player to the ball calls a colour to choose a teammate. They play a 2v1 against the other player.

A goal is scored by dribbling through the poles.

3. Technical — Crossing and Heading Practice with 4 Goals — 20 mins

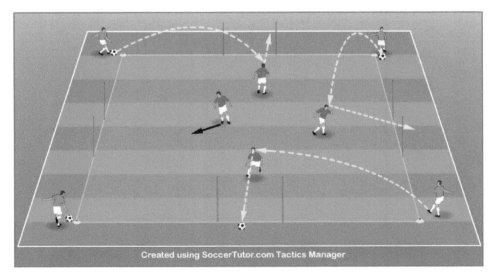

Description

In an area 20 x 20 yards, we have 4 goals at the sides.

In the corners there are 4 players that cross the ball into the playing area where 4 players will try to head the ball into one of the goals.

Coaching Points

1. The timing of the cross and the run needs to be coordinated.
2. Get the players to use different types of headers during this practice

4. Game Situation — Crossing and Heading Team Game
20 mins

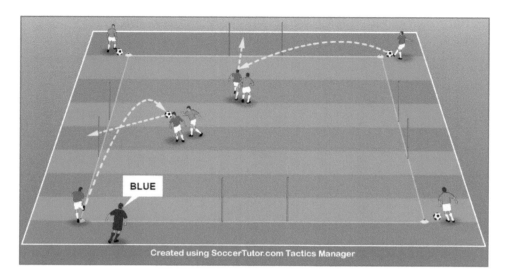

Created using SoccerTutor.com Tactics Manager

Description

We reduce the size of the square from the last practice to 15 x 15 yards.

In the corners there are 4 players with 1 ball each (2 balls per team).

On the coach's call the players in the corner will cross the ball to their teammates, resulting in a 2v2 game and the goal must be scored with a header.

Coaching Points

1. In this progression from the last practice, the players need to check away from their marker before making the run to head at goal.

2. The player crossing the ball needs to display good awareness and timing to meet the runs.

5. Specific Game — Shooting from Distance with 6 Goals in a 3 Zone Small Sided Game
20 mins

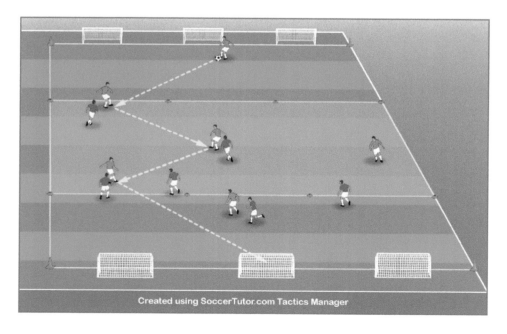

Created using SoccerTutor.com Tactics Manager

Description

Using half a full size pitch, we play a 6v6 game.

The players can move freely across all zones, but can only shoot from within the central zone.

The defending team have to be able to defend all the 3 goals.

Variations

1. A goal is only valid if the shot is hit along the ground.

2. A goal is only valid from an aerial shot.

Practice 6   Free Small Sided Game
20 mins

SESSION
45

Individual Tactical Objective: Positioning to defend the goal.

Group Tactical Objective: Collective movements when in possession of the ball.

Technical Objective: Heading.

Motor Athletic Objective: Quickness.

Duration of Session: 110 minutes

We recommend starting the session with exercises for general mobility to prevent injuries.

| **1. Warm Up** | **Jump, Criss-Cross and Heading Competition** | **20 mins** |

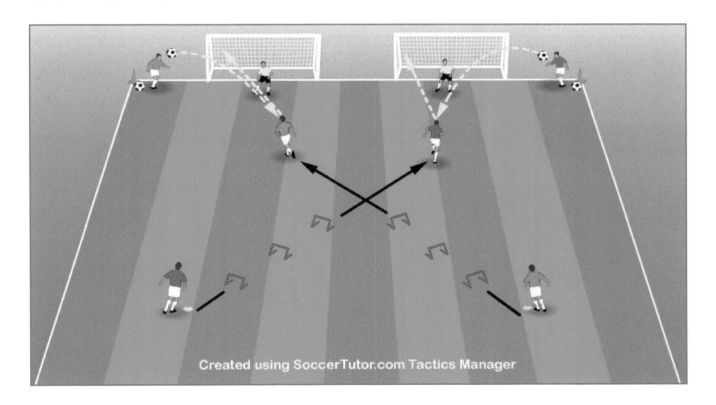

Created using SoccerTutor.com Tactics Manager

Description

2 teams compete in this game.

One player stands next to the goal and throws-in for their teammate to head the ball in the goal.

The heading player first jumps over the hurdles and sprints diagonally to meet the throw.

The team that scores the most goals win.

2. Conditioning — Running Through Poles and Volley
10 mins

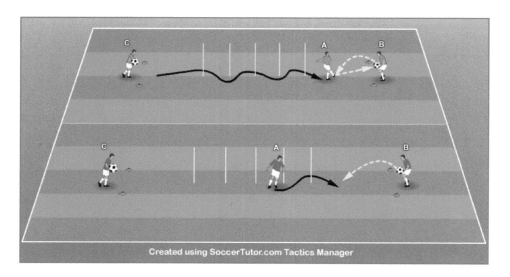

Description

Players A runs in and out of the poles without the ball and then volley passes the ball to a teammate (player B) who has thrown them the ball.

B and A then swap positions and player B repeats the same process in the other direction towards player C.

3. Technical — Defensive Positioning to Block the Shot
20 mins

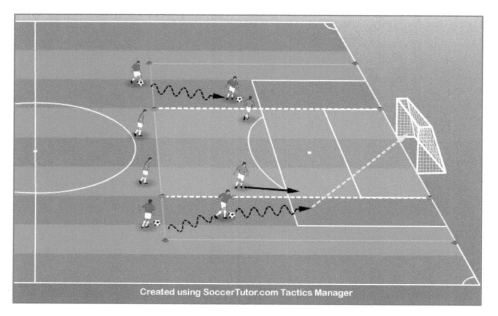

Description

The blue player has the objective to score by shooting.

The red player must cover the shooting path and try to block the shot.

Both players are separated by a line into their separate zones and cannot come into contact.

Coaching Points

1. The correct positioning and body shape of the defender is needed to close off the shooting angle.
2. The attacking player needs to dribble at full speed to create an angle or space to shoot into the goal.

4. Game Situation — Collective Tactical Movement — 20 mins

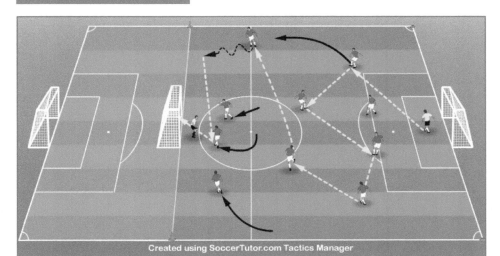

Description

Set out the team according to their usual formation.

Players must perform movements appropriate when in possession of the ball.

The players build up play from the back and end with finishing on goal.

Coaching Points

1. Make sure the players pass and move at full speed so they best replicate a real game.

2. The build up play should vary greatly each time using different combination play.

5. Specific Game — 6v6 with 6 Outside Support Players — 20 mins

Description

Players can only play with their heads and can use the outside support players.

When the ball hits the ground possession changes hands.

Practice 6   Free Small Sided Game — 20 mins

ADDITIONAL STRENGTH, ENDURANCE AND SPEED PRACTICES

Strength & Power Practices

Practice 1 Jumping and Volley Pass Circuit

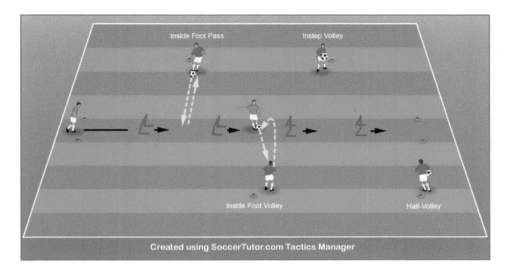

Description

The hurdles are approximately 2 yards away from each other.

The players must jump over the hurdles and perform a different type of volley in between them (inside of the foot pass along the ground, instep volley and a half volley).

Practice 2 Crossing and Heading on the Run

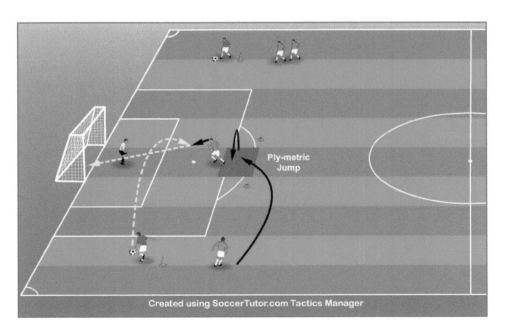

Description

The red player runs around and through the cones, climbs onto the blue block, performs a plymetric jump and heads the ball at goal which is crossed by the blue player on the flank.

Practice 3   Juggling in Pairs

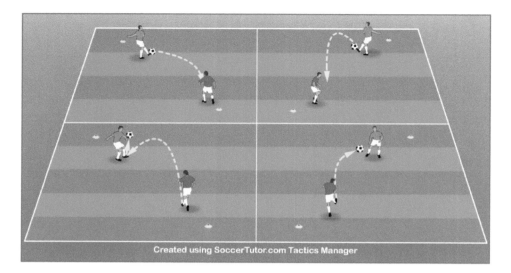

Description

Players juggle the ball and after they pass the ball to the other player, they sit on the ground and get up without the use of their hands before receiving again.

Practice 4   Dynamic Technical Circuit

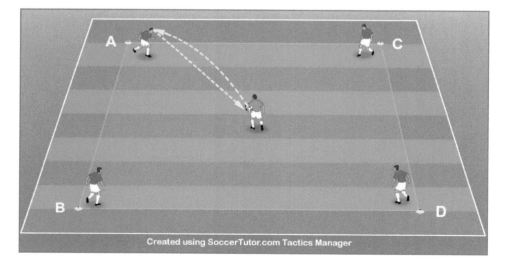

Description

Set up 4 stations where players perform different exercises:

1. Heading

2. Laying with back on the ground, the player gets up and volley passes.

3. Laying on the ground on their front, they get up and volley pass.

4. From a sitting position, the player gets up without using their hands and volley passes.

Practice 5 Strengthening Exercises and 1v1 Duels

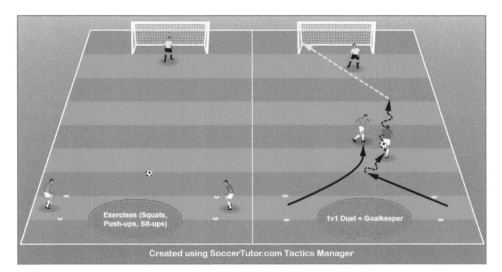

Exercises (Squats, Push-ups, Sit-ups)

1v1 Duel + Goalkeeper

Created using SoccerTutor.com Tactics Manager

Description

2 players on the side of the field perform various strengthening exercises (squats, push-ups, sit-ups).

Each exercise must be repeated 8-10 times and afterwards the players get to play in a 1v1 game trying to score in the goal past the goalkeeper.

Practice 6 Strength Exercises Relay

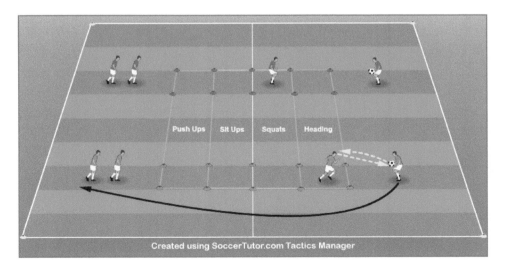

Push Ups   Sit Ups   Squats   Heading

Created using SoccerTutor.com Tactics Manager

Description

Station 1: Push ups

Station 2: Sit ups

Station 3: Squats

Station 4: Heading the ball back to the teammate who throws it up in the air.

The next player then goes.

Players perform 8 to 10 repetitions per station

Endurance Practices

Practice 1   Endurance Possession Game

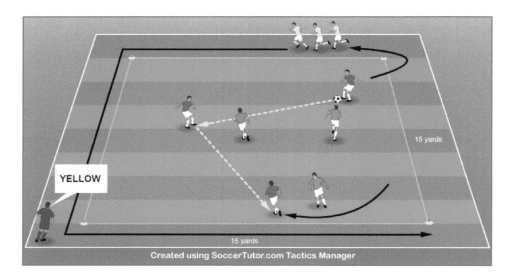

Description

The coach calls out the colour of the team whose players must run around the field 3 times at high speed.

At the same time, the 2 teams inside the square will play a possession game. The team that completes the most passes wins the game.

Play for 5 minutes with 2 minutes recovery time.

Practice 2   Changing Direction and Dribbling at Speed

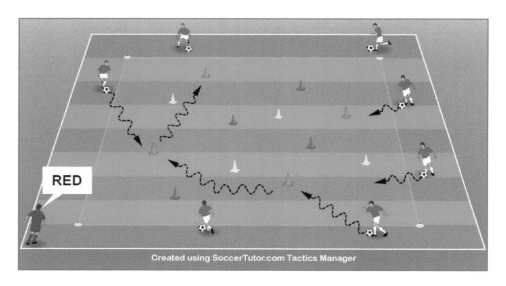

Description

Players dribble around the square at a relaxed pace.

When the coach calls out a colour the players must dribble at maximum speed towards the colour cone called out.

The coach will call out the colours in quick succession

Practice 3　3v3 High Intensity Small Sided Game

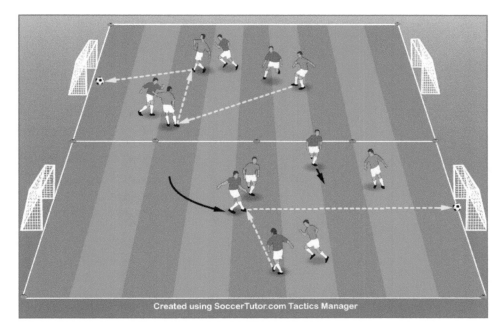

Description

In a small area, players play a 3v3 game with the aim of constantly keeping the ball moving and in play.

As soon as the ball goes out of play, the coach needs to immediately pass another ball into play.

Practice 4　Closing Down and Winning the Ball (1v5)

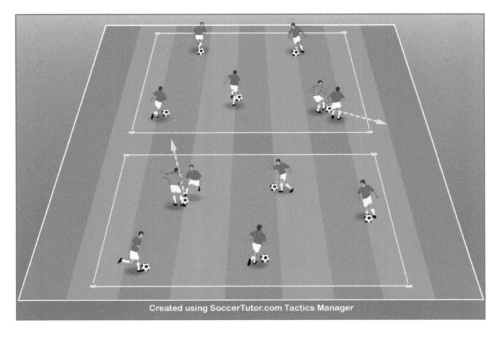

Description

Here we have 5 players in a narrow area (rectangle) with a ball each.

The red player (who does not have a ball must try to kick the other players balls' out of play.

The last player with a ball wins.

Practice 5   Possession Circle with Coloured Defenders

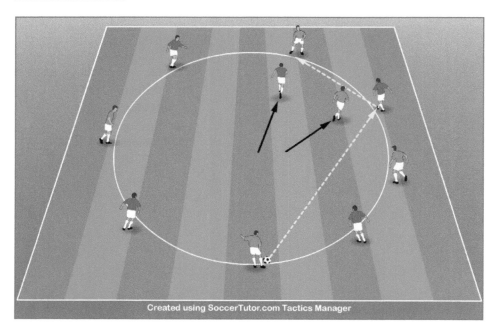

Created using SoccerTutor.com Tactics Manager

Description

Players are divided into 2 colours and form a circle with 2 players in the middle (1 of each colour).

The red player can only close down other red players and the blue player can only close down the blue players.

The players in the middle work intensely for 1 minute before changing roles with a teammate.

Practice 6   Quick Reactions 1v1 Duel Game

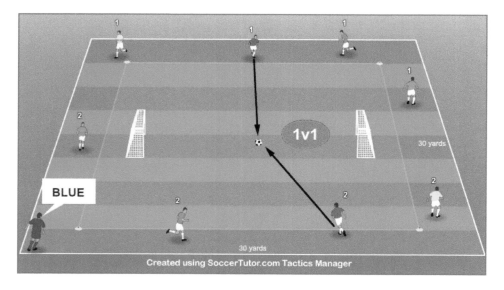

1v1

30 yards

30 yards

BLUE

Created using SoccerTutor.com Tactics Manager

Description

In this practice 8 players wear 4 different colours and are assigned with number 1 or 2.

All the players run around the outside of the 30 x 30 yard square.

When the coach calls out a colour, the players run into the middle to get to the ball first and play a 1v1. They then go back to the outside and we carry on.

Speed Practices

Quick Reactions to Change the Direction of Play in a SSG

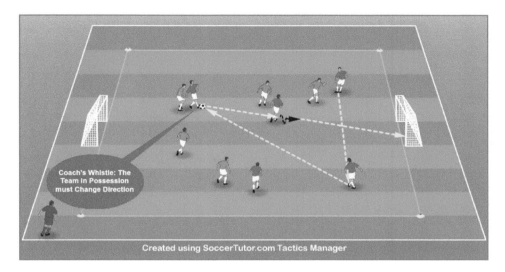

Coach's Whistle: The Team in Possession must Change Direction

Created using SoccerTutor.com Tactics Manager

Description

This game is played in a small area.

On the coach's whistle, the team in possession must quickly change direction and attack the opposite goal.

Vary the timing of the whistle.

Practice 2   Dribbling Shadow Play

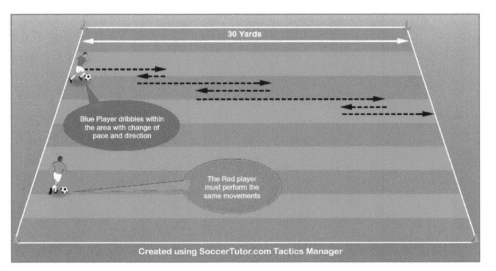

30 Yards

Blue Player dribbles within the area with change of pace and direction

The Red player must perform the same movements

Created using SoccerTutor.com Tactics Manager

Description

The blue player dribbles the ball within a 30 yard space and constantly changes the pace and direction.

The red player must have good awareness to copy the exact same movements.

Practice 3 | Sprinting with Quick Reactions

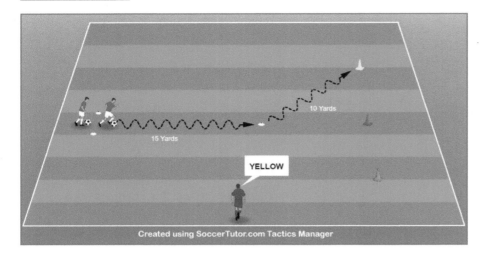

Description

The player sprints with the ball for 15 yards and then the coach calls out a colour. The player then must sprint another 10 yards to the colour cone called out.

Variations

1. Change the sequence of the colours.
2. Call out 2 colours where the players cannot sprint to.

Practice 4 | Speed of Reaction 1v1 Duel

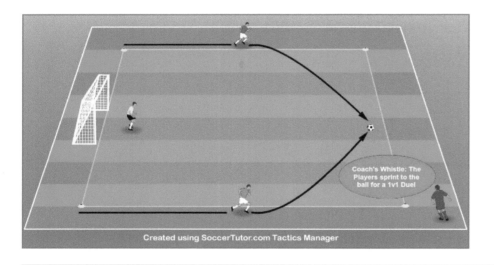

Description

Both players sprint at maximum speed and wait for the coach's whistle.

As soon as they hear the coach's whistle, they can enter the field and race to the ball to play in a 1v1.

Practice 5 | Acceleration in a 2v1 Duel

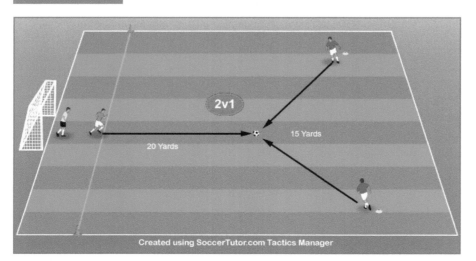

Description

Starting from a standing position, 2 attackers and 1 defender sprint to the ball and play a 2v1 game.

The attackers start 15 yards away from the ball at an angle and the defender has a 20 yard straight run to the ball.

Practice 6 — Acceleration and Deceleration Exercise

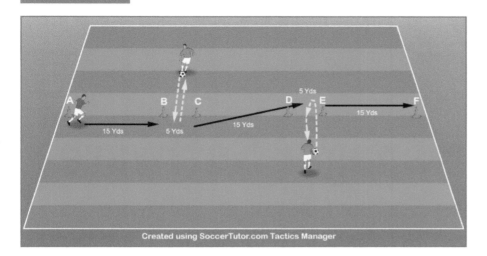

Description

Starting from a standing position, the player sprints from A to B (15 yards). Between B and C the player decelerates and plays a pass back to their teammate.

The player sprints again from C to D and plays a volley pass between D and E. The exercises finishes with a final sprint from E to F. x

Practice 7 — Acceleration and Deceleration in a 1v1 Duel

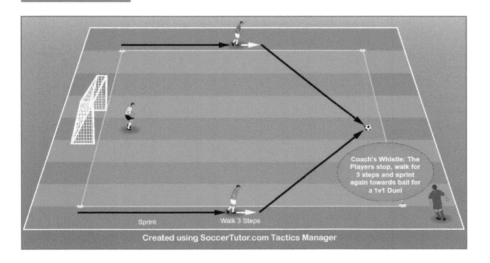

Description

Players A and B sprint at maximum speed.

On the coach's whistle they stop, walk for 3 steps and sprint again towards the ball.

The 2 players then compete in a 1v1 duel.

Practice 8 — Acceleration, Deceleration and Speed of Reaction

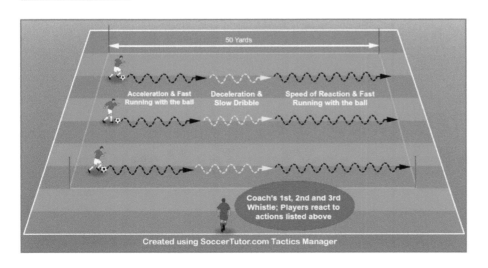

Description

Players run with the ball over a 50 yard distance at maximum speed.

On the coach's whistle, they stop and start again with a slower dribble. At the next whistle, they start sprinting again to run with the ball at maximum speed.

The whistles are repeated for the whole length of the run to set the tempo.

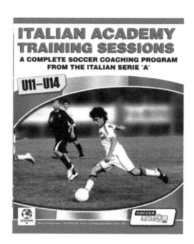